=GARBO=

GARBO

A PORTRAIT BY ALEXANDER WALKER
AUTHORIZED BY METRO-GOLDWYN-MAYER

MACMILLAN PUBLISHING CO., INC.
NEW YORK

FOR STANLEY KUBRICK

Macmillan Publishing Co., Inc.
866 Third Avenue, New York, N.Y. 10022
Collier Macmillan Canada, Ltd.

Library of Congress Cataloging in Publication Data
Walker, Alexander, film critic
   Garbo.

   Bibliography: p.
   Filmography: p.
   Includes index.
   1. Garbo, Greta, 1905–   2. Moving-picture actors
   and actresses–Sweden–Biography.   I. Metro-Goldwyn-Mayer, inc.
PN2778.G3W3   791.43′028′0924 [B]   80-12717
ISBN 0-02-622950-1

Designed by John Gorham and Martin Richards

10 9 8 7 6 5 4 3 2 1

Printed in Great Britain

CONTENTS

c./M

INTRODUCTION

AS IN THE CASE of many books, the desire to write this one arrived long before the opportunity. What I had in mind could not have been written without a fortuitous meeting with Frank E. Rosenfelt. In the course of half-an-hour's drive with this shrewd, amiable man down to Pinewood Studios – where he was going to view the shooting of one of his company's films and I to interview its director – I found the President and Chief Executive of Metro-Goldwyn-Mayer, Inc. to be an ardent movie buff as well as a corporation head. He told me how, one evening, he had taken some of the Greta Garbo files out of the studio archives, to check some point that was relevant to contemporary projects, and sat engrossed till well past his suppertime just turning back through all the contracts, letters, cables and memoranda between studio executives and craftsmen who had the custody, care and tensions of Garbo's career as their responsibility. 'Would you ever,' I said, 'let a film historian look over your shoulder . . .?'

Within weeks, a letter from MGM, at Culver City on the American west coast, indicated that I would be a welcome researcher – and there was no need to go in for over-the-shoulder 'kibbitzing'. Every bit of Garbo material still in the studio's possession was brought at my request, willingly and surprisingly dust-free. Before I even sought the answers to questions I had formulated, one thing impressed me: the care that a major studio like MGM has taken to preserve what could be called its corporate memory in the shape of records that went back in this case nearly sixty years. Even when I unexpectedly called for files on Mauritz Stiller or John Gilbert, they were produced without delay. I had freedom to read through them and make notes from them in the MGM law library, almost next door to the famous office where Louis B. Mayer held court and from which, periodically, Frank Rosenfelt would emerge, padding by to the conference room, but drawn in magnetically to peer over *my* shoulder and ask, 'What have you found . . what have you found?'. The idea that a studio spurns its past unless there is profit to be made from it is not one that has any place at MGM. I also made another, more gradual discovery, worth noting for other historians of cinema. Though corporate heads may change quickly in today's Hollywood – and some of them roll off the chopping block – there is a sort of 'permanent civil service' heading the many other departments of a studio; and these people go on from one decade to another and often seem to be as much the repository of valuable evidence about the movies as the actual documents themselves. This is so at MGM, where I began finding among the later Garbo papers the initialled memoranda of (then) relatively junior employees who, at the time of my researches, were occupying senior posts – all of thirty or thirty-five years later. I had only to walk a few yards, stick my head through so-and-so's door and tap their memory – invariably good – to gain insight on some point that had baffled me earlier in the written record.

I must add one other thing: in spite of giving me complete freedom to browse and quote, MGM asked for no contractual right to see what I proposed to publish, and no personal request was made to me for an advance look at the typescript. Any opinions that I arrived at are therefore very much my own and I accept the responsibility for them, and for any inadvertent errors I may have made.

It seems to me that more than enough has already been written in the last two decades, when the dam waters broke and film books flowed in torrential numbers out of publishing houses the world over, about the 'outside view' of the movies. That is to say, the view formed by piecing together evidence in the shape of films, reviews and oral testimony (both hearsay and direct). I have contributed to this outpouring myself in earlier books. But if film history is going to be revised and refreshed in the present decade, then it can only be done if the great studios are as generous with their company papers as MGM has been to me and a few fellow researchers in their past history. We badly need material we can depend on, which means records that have not been revised with hindsight and reports that are not dependent on frail memory or, sometimes, sturdier wishful thinking. The day-to-day transactions of the studio business is where the next strike ought to be made, provided it is undertaken as responsible archaeology and not an unregulated gold rush.

This book draws heavily and, I hope, revealingly on the MGM archives to give an insight into the power-play of a major studio and its greatest star over sixteen years. As its subtitle indicates, it is 'a portrait', an impression of Garbo as her life, career and temperament shaped, and were shaped by, her personality and talents. The self-imposed limits preclude a full-scale biography. Other books of mine seek to throw critical light on Garbo's screen performances. In this account I have given more weight and space to what the archives disclosed or suggested, and tried to deduce from this evidence the changing personality as well as the professional aggrandizement of the star. The illustrations have been a powerful supplementary tool and I trust they will be 'read' in the context of the narrative for the light they throw on the extraordinary facets of this woman. The question will undoubtedly be asked: have I ever met her? Yes, is the answer, though in circumstances that would not have allowed for much inquiry into the material I found elsewhere, even supposing she had been willing or able to assist me. Disappointing, yes; dismaying, no. In a way, I am glad she keeps her distance, and her mystery. My only lively regret is an apprehension of all the uncorroborated personal memories that will assuredly spill out into print when Garbo is no longer here, able to deter such authors and, in the absence of her own version, to give her life the protection of the truth as she sees it.

I am grateful to many people who assisted me. Some who are, or have been, close to Garbo have asked that I do not name them. Others I gladly acknowledge, particularly those at Metro-Goldwyn-Mayer. In addition to Frank Rosenfelt, I should like to thank Richard Kahn, senior vice-president and worldwide head of marketing, motion-picture division, and president of MGM International; Deanna Rae Wilcox, director of marketing management services; Karla Davidson, associate general counsel; Herbert Nusbaum, attorney, MGM; Florence Warner, office manager, legal department; Doré Freeman, head of stills; Ben Presser, head of legal files; and Iver Person, who helped me prepare the frame enlargements from the Garbo films. They were all generous in rendering me assistance and scrupulous in leaving me to my own devices.

In Los Angeles, I would also like to thank the staff of the Margaret Herrick Library at the Academy of Motion Picture Arts and Sciences, and in particular Sam Gill, for their assistance with the illustrations and immediate access to the rich collection of MGM stills deposited by the company at the Academy during my researches – an invaluable collection of source material.

In Stockholm, I was assisted by Olle Rosberg, head of photographic stills at the Swedish Film Institute; Torsten Jungstedt, who ran much television material for my inspection; Jorn Donner, director, Swedish Film Institute; Bengt Forslund, production chief, Swedish Film Institute; Kenne Fant, director-general, Svensk Filmindustri; Ture Sjölander, author and designer; the picture library staffs at Pressens Bild and the Bonnier publishing group and Allan Kjellander; and especially Sven Gustafsson, nephew of Greta Garbo, who dealt warmly and fairly with my inquiries and allowed me to reproduce photos from his private collection.

In London I was helped by Bill Edwards, vice-president, advertising and publicity of MGM International; the staff at the British Film Institute reference library and the National Film Archive stills department; and, it almost goes without saying, Kevin Brownlow.

My publishers deserve my warm thanks for their encouragement and patience. For the enthusiasm they displayed throughout the project, I especially thank Colin Webb, director, art and illustrated books; Brigid Avison, my editor and picture researcher; and John Gorham and Martin Richards, who designed the book.

Alexander Walker
London 1979 – Davos 1980

Greta Gustafsson aged seventeen: 'Whenever I am left to myself, I long
so dreadfully for the theatre.'

GRETA GUSTAFSSON
1905-1925

LOUIS B. MAYER had personally ordered her to report to the studio. But when morning and afternoon came and went, and Greta Garbo did not appear, a messenger was sent out to her at the Miramar Hotel, Santa Monica, on the Californian coast. He delivered his letter, then prudently waited for a signed receipt which was stapled to the carbon copy on his return to the Metro-Goldwyn-Mayer studios at Culver City, a suburb of Los Angeles. Both have been preserved in the company's well-ordered files. So, too, has the tone of patriarchal rebuke administered over fifty years ago, on 5 November 1926, by one of the most irresistible forces among the Hollywood moguls to a girl who had just turned twenty-one, had been barely a year in his employment and was about to prove herself, in temperamental obduracy at least, the film colony's most immovable object.

'Yesterday you were notified by telephone as well as by letter to report to our studio this morning at the hour of ten o'clock a.m.,' Mayer began. Then he let the thunder roll. 'You have disobeyed this instruction and we have not heard from you either directly or indirectly. In view of this situation and considering particularly the shortage of time left to us before commencing the photographing of the photoplay *Women Love Diamonds*, which was to be your next vehicle, it will be impossible for us to cast you in the picture. We desire you to know at this time that it is our intention to engage another artist to play the part assigned

to you.' Garbo's grasp of English was still extremely shaky. But when this was translated into Swedish for her, it is doubtful whether she considered it heart-wrenching news. The part in question had been described by the impenitent culprit herself a few days before as that of 'a stupid seductress'. Stupid or not, Mayer warned her icily that 'careful search and preparation will be necessary to find another suitable vehicle for you and to prepare same for production. This may require a considerable period of time during which it may be impossible for us to use your services, and in such an event your resulting idleness would be due purely to your attitude and to your wilful disobedience of instructions.'

Then the whip was cracked, as it was to be many, many times in those early star-taming sessions which long-term contracts were making inevitable in the burgeoning studio system of the mid-1920s.

'Until further notice you are instructed to report daily to our studio at the hour of nine o'clock a.m. Failure on your part to comply with the provisions of this notice will be deemed to constitute a wilful disregard of your obligations under your contract of employment with us and during the period of any insubordination on your part your compensation under said contract will be terminated.' Despite

Louis B. Mayer, Garbo, Lars Hanson and Sven-Hugo Borg on the set of *Flesh and the Devil* in 1926.

MGM-3586

the righteous itch he no doubt felt to call a recalcitrant and (he considered) ungrateful star to heel, Mayer ended his letter on a note of corporate self-protection. 'It is not our intention by the service of this notice to terminate your contract of employment with us, but on the contrary we desire to emphasize the fact that we consider the same in full force and effect and shall do everything in our power to compel the strict and faithful performance by you of your obligations thereunder. Yours very truly, Metro-Goldwyn-Mayer Corporation, Louis B. Mayer, Vice-President.' A duplicate letter was despatched eastwards to Joseph S. Buhler, Garbo's lawyer in New York.

A careful but anonymous hand, practised in the minutiae that regulated life in what was then the most efficiently managed studio in Hollywood, has noted down on the MGM archive copy the exact hour of the day when this thunderbolt was hurled – 7.00 p.m. Louis B. Mayer had barely let the sun set on his displeasure with a woman who had up to then made only three films for him (one of them as yet unseen), but was about to be hailed by critics and filmgoers alike as 'divine'. Over the next fifteen years, Mayer was to see Garbo in many lights – but never this one.

Garbo in 1926 was fast learning the difference between being an artist and becoming an asset. Her contrariness had already caught Mayer's watchful eye. 'Always the vamp I am, always the woman of no heart,' she complained after only two films, *The Torrent* and *The Temptress*. Mayer had written her, on 4 August 1926, the first of those curt letters ordering her to report, at 4.30 p.m. precisely, to his production chief Irving Thalberg 'to receive instructions on *Flesh and the Devil*'. In this she was to play yet another heartless 'vamp', ironically named Felicitas. Garbo tried unsuccessfully to turn it down. Failing, she then tried to obtain a wardrobe for her role in it, Mayer noted, 'in a manner other than intimated by us' – which expressed his studio's iron-clad concern for going by the book. Mayer put it bluntly: 'Failure on your part to comply with this demand, particularly in view of the attitude heretofore displayed by you, and your general insubordination, will be treated as a breach of your contract.' Garbo did not report as instructed: she sent a message saying she was ill. A handwritten note in ink on Mayer's memo records that she was accordingly suspended without pay for eight days. She was told that the time spent on suspension would be added to the three-year contract she had signed with MGM on 16 August 1925. The lay-off cost her $400 – her weekly rate at the time.

Nothing illustrates Garbo's 'worth', in one sense at least, more ruthlessly than a memo sent to Mayer and Thalberg by one of the studio's production managers. It shows stardom stripped down to naked accountancy. 'For year September 10, 1925, to September 9, 1926: worked in MGM pictures 12 and 4/6 weeks at $400 a week. Total: $4,922.33. Lay-off taken: 12 weeks. Balance of contract 15 and 1/6 weeks at $400 a week. Total: $6,066.66. Total salary paid: $16,066.66. Paid for idle time: $4,933.33. Plus salary from May 27 till September 9, 1926. Total: $6,066.66 – if idle to the end of term, this will amount to $10,999.99.' The memo adds: 'We have a further option for a year at $750 a week.'

Not long after this was circulated, Garbo was acting opposite John Gilbert, a star whose remuneration was nearly $10,000 a week. To her artistic dissatisfaction was added a more materialistic concern: she was underpriced.

'They are mean,' she wrote home at this time to a Swedish friend. 'They' were also far-sighted. Louis B. Mayer again suspended Garbo when she ignored his rebuke and refused to report to the studio daily: she was absent for forty-three days until 17 December 1926. During this time a memo circulated among the executives concerning the action open to the studio if Garbo decided to go back to Sweden, or invited deportation by refusing to apply for an extension of her work permit. 'Our attorney would take the opinion that we had a valid and lasting contract and would have recourse to several points of law in enforcing the contract (if the artist later returned to the United States). He says we could make it very unpleasant for such a person, with the possibility of preventing working for others.' The person's gender is not specified: there was no need. Mayer had sent for Garbo in mid-November and openly taxed her with ingratitude.

No record of this confrontation has survived. But Mayer's compulsive paternalism, part affectionate parent, part retributive tyrant, had been solidly fixed by then. Any one of the well-attested speeches he was fond of making about his 'family' of stars would have applied. 'Only Garbo is difficult. I am her best friend. I want her to be happy. She should come and tell me about what she wants. I'd talk her out of it.'[1] This time, anyhow, Garbo told Mayer exactly what she wanted. She wanted her salary raised to $5,000 a week. And she was not going to be talked out of it. She went home and stayed there for five months, on no pay.

The only way of penetrating the mystery that has gathered around Greta Garbo in the fifty-odd years since this confrontation with Mayer is to assume that it does not exist. This is why I have quoted, without delay, from the remarkable cache of memoranda, letters, contracts and other items deposited in the vaults at the MGM studios. Some people might consider such an approach to be anti-romantic, even anti-Garbo. I can only ask them to postpone judgment. Personally, I find it an essential corrective to the myth that was even then forming around Garbo, on and off-screen. The myth has enjoyed such a long tenure, and formed people's view of her, that it is high time one sought a new perspective on its subject. The MGM document files permit us to do this.

Going through them as I did, in the law library at MGM, is not an exercise in disenchantment: rather the reverse. They fill in some of the fascinating conundrums in Garbo's career. If one knows how to formulate the questions, these papers suggest some of the answers. What they do not disperse is the essential mystery of Garbo's personality, though they furnish firmer grounds for speculating about some aspects of it. And they do nothing at all to destroy her uniqueness. If anything, they enhance it by reminding us that, at the very least, there were two kinds of truth about Greta Garbo. There is the truth to be found in her performances, in the display of her personality on screen. And there is the truth that has been committed to print in the company records covering her MGM career from 1925 to 1941. One truth provides the material for celebration and critical analysis: the other provides the evidence about some of the external forces that shape a star. What the MGM files remind us is that before there was a 'divine' Garbo, there was a woman subjected to the same laws of reward and punishment as a score or more of her famous contemporaries who did not have any claim to divinity made for them in their screen lifetime, or thereafter.

The turn of 1926–7 was the growth-time of the Garbo who would very soon be assuming her fugitive and enduring mystery. But the studio archives allow us to achieve another view of her throughout her career. In a word, they let us see Garbo plain.

Other stars have aped Garbo's remoteness, her refusal amounting to an obsession to let admirers identify with her, or even set eyes on her, except as a screen image – and ultimately she was to deny them even that satisfaction by giving up making films altogether. But no star has so convincingly, tenaciously or continuously exhibited her strength of will in protecting her essential self, even at the risk of a unique film career. The early years at MGM were the forcing-bed of her egotism: but it pre-dates them. The stamp of wilfulness is on Garbo from early childhood, her most trenchant characteristic. All the trustworthy reports of that period, including some of her own, refer to one thing – a determination to make her will prevail.

The youngest of three children, she was born in a Stockholm maternity home on 18 September 1905. The family, named Gustafsson, already had a son, Sven, and a daughter, Alva. Garbo's given names were Greta Lovisa. Her father, Karl Alfred, did some low-paid work in the city scavenging department which took him out in all weathers, exposed him to the hazards of the alcoholic 'tips' that Stockholmers gave to street-cleaners in those days, and probably weakened his not very sturdy constitution still further. He was a man of astonishingly delicate features, almost feminine – these Garbo inherited. He had met her mother, Anna Lovisa, on a farm where he was an outdoor labourer and she was a kitchen-maid. There was a hint of Lapp blood on Garbo's mother's side: she was a kind woman, but taciturn. It is tempting to see her genes in her younger daughter's long limbs, flat chest and yoke of collar-bone broad enough to harness shire horses. An ungainly body in repose, it was the way that Garbo's torso and lower limbs meshed sensuously together when she moved, imparting a stalking motion, that made a vividly physical impression on the first American audiences who saw her. It may be this directness of attack that caused

ABOVE Her mother, a sturdy peasant with Lapp blood.

RIGHT The imposing tenement façade at 32, Blekingegatan; but Greta's family was confined to a cramped flat at the rear.

people to believe her stature was Amazonian. Not so: when she filed her application for US citizenship in the 1940s, she gave her height as five feet seven inches, hardly a giantess. The old canard about her 'excessive' height probably persists because some of her leading men, like John Gilbert or Charles Boyer, were comparatively small or wore historical costumes that further diminished them. Watch how often, as Marie Walewska playing opposite Boyer's Napoleon, she has to risk *lèse-majesté* in the Emperor's presence by leaning against a table or chair, knees slightly bent, so as to allow him his imperial inches.

Soon after Garbo's birth, her family moved to a tenement apartment at 32, Blekingegatan. The building no longer exists, but a Swedish television film made at the time of its demolition suggests that Garbo's upbringing was cramped and unhealthy. If the large windows let in the fresh air, they also admitted wintry winds. The family slept five to a room, Greta in the middle on a camp bed. An oven boiled the water, baked the food and dried the fire-wood. The lavatory was across an outside courtyard; and it was on the gently sloping roofs of it and its neighbours that Greta used to sunbathe or day-dream with her intimates. Her friends' memories, in so far as they are not coloured by wishful association with her celebrity, suggest the kind of lonely child who imposes her inward picture of things upon everyday reality. She was the shyest of the children, already showing signs of withdrawal, which she would later turn into so potent a weapon, by hugging one corner of the living-room. But with friends her own age, she always took the lead in games, preferring soldiers to dolls, and to one girl, Elizabeth Malcolm, 'she was a show in herself'.

'We are on a sandy white beach,' Greta would say [as the two girls lay on the lavatory roofs]. 'Can't you see the waves breaking on the shore? How clear the sky is, Elizabeth! And do you hear how sweetly that orchestra at the Casino is playing? Look at that girl in the funny green bathing suit! It's fun to lie here and look at the

bathers, isn't it?' [Her] vivid imagination had no difficulty in transforming the tin roof into a glistening beach, the backyard with its clothes lines and ash cans into a windswept ocean, the raspy gramophone music floating through some neighbour's open window into sweet melodies from a fashionable casino orchestra. The children shouting in the yard were, of course, the bathers.[2]

Years later, in a rare Hollywood interview, virtually the last in which she opened her thoughts to outsiders for publication, Garbo said of this time: 'I can't remember being young, really young, like other children.' And she added one of the most telling self-comments ever recorded: 'I always had my opinions, but I never told my mind.' She said that even as a child she wanted to be alone. She used to crawl into a corner and think things over. 'Children should be allowed to think when they please; they should not be molested. "Go and play now," their mothers and fathers tell them. They shouldn't do that. Thinking means so much even to small children.'[3]

Garbo was not an energetic child. Possibly she did not have the physical stamina for tobogganing, snowballing or the other winter-time games. She did her playing by thinking, by pretending, a game that incorporates an unusually high number of 'ups' and 'downs'. 'Very happy one moment: the next, there was nothing left for me.' At school, she was a bright girl, but undirected. What fascinated her was not lessons, but the live theatre. She claimed that when six or seven years of age she used to stand outside the back door of one of Stockholm's two dozen theatres and listen to the actors playing parts in shows she could not afford to see. When she could pay for a seat, or was treated to a night at the play, the experience inspired her to paint her face with water-colours in lieu of greasepaint and, on occasion, to put on her brother Sven's breeches and shirt and venture into the neighbourhood to see which of the tradesmen would be taken in by the local child *en transvestie*.

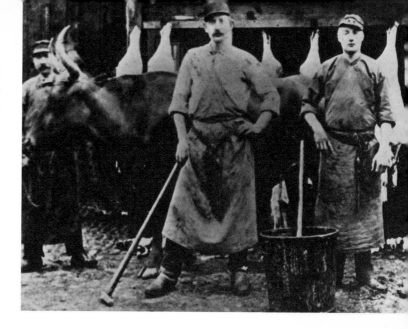

The silent cinema, being cheaper, pulled her in even oftener than the live theatre. She doted on Mary Pickford and saw *Poor Little Rich Girl* at least twice, comprehending and enjoying the artifice that enabled Pickford, a young woman of twenty-four when she made the film in 1917, to pass for a little girl of eleven. Elizabeth Malcolm has said that this prompted Garbo to ask why she, who *was* a little girl, then about twelve or thirteen, should not do as well as Pickford on the screen. The two of them tried walking out to the film studios on Lidingö island, in a Stockholm suburb, but the search for film fame foundered in a snowstorm: no one could direct them to where they had no doubt their careers as film stars were waiting.

Of bleaker record in Garbo's memory is the death of her father when she was about fourteen. The family had nursed him through illness contracted during the world-wide influenza epidemic of 1919. S. N. Behrman, the playwright and screenwriter of (amongst other films) *Ninotchka*, has recalled how Garbo told him that her father called her in one day in May 1920, saying he felt very sick. Finding him burning with fever, she took him to a public clinic where they had to stand in line. When they finally got to the window, the man told Karl Gustafsson to take off his hat and asked a hundred questions, all seeming to indicate to him and the small girl that the hospital was principally interested in their ability to pay for treatment. All this time, Garbo felt her father almost dying by her side; according to her, he did die a few days later. Behrman said the incident at the hospital was one source of fury that Garbo held against life. It probably taught her, painfully early in life, that having money was the best protection, and being chary about how she spent it was added insurance. Behrman also believed that, by some nagging connection, she associated 'officialdom', in the later personage of Louis B. Mayer, with the peremptory, uncaring 'man at the window'.

Her father crops up in another story that still finds its way into the biographies, though it belongs in the Garbo apocrypha. It relates how one night she came on her father fighting another man in the street and getting the worst of it – until the fight stopped when she was recognized as his daughter. But as Garbo herself recalled, the fight did not

ABOVE Greta's father (right) at work as a farm hand.

LEFT Greta (top centre) at school, aged about nine.

involve her parent. She simply asked the bigger man why he was fighting and, looking down at his worsted opponent, the man said sarcastically, 'Here's your little daughter – you can go home now.' Parent or not, the sight taught Garbo to fear physical violence, especially any that risked involving her. Hence her lifelong antipathy to crowds of strangers, even film extras on a studio set where a Garbo 'double' was sometimes substituted in long shots if she had to appear in their midst. Most film stars overcome or contain their aversion to the multitude; not she.

During her father's illness, she had already been contributing to the family budget by working after school hours as lather-girl in a backstreet barber's shop. Memories of her in those days suggest a lively girl who 'chatted up' the clients. But being exposed to the fairly uninhibited talk of working-class men may have given her a basic, far from reassuring insight into the male sex. If this is supposition, a matter of record are the insecurities that showed up in her close and jealous friendships with other girls in their mid-teens. One of her biographers, the Swedish actor Fritiof Billquist, reproduced excerpts from letters written by the fourteen-year-old Greta to her schoolfriend Eva Blomkvist. These make astonishing and disconcerting reading: they are painfully self-analytical, so obviously the product of a lonely child's introspection. They are also very headstrong in tone: words are not wasted, thoughts not restrained. The traits are clearly those

LEFT During her last year in school, about to become the family breadwinner.

BELOW With her confirmation class in 1920. Greta Gustafsson is top centre.

OPPOSITE In her confirmation dress, just twelve days after her father's death. Feelings already had to be borne silently.

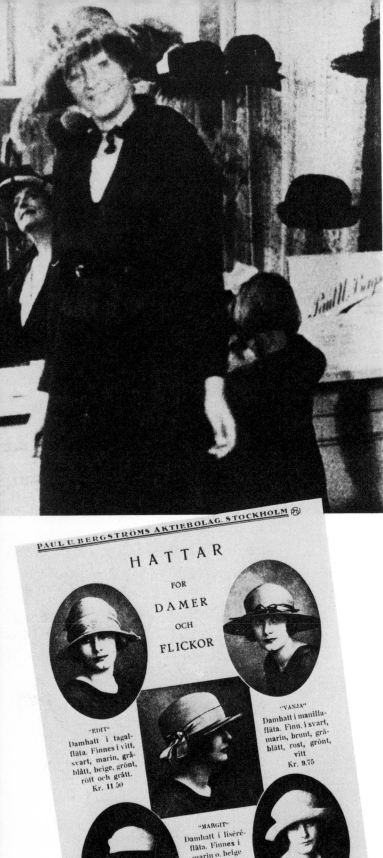

of a girl determined to get her own way, whatever the price she pays in suffering. It is the first undoubted intimation of the Garbo temperament.

'I did not mind your going out with [my sister] Alva,' Garbo writes, 'but I realized you intended to do the same with all my acquaintances. Eva, I am arrogant and impatient by nature and I don't like girls who do what you have done. If you hadn't written, I should never have made the first move towards reconciliation. . . . If this letter offends you, then you don't need to write to me again, but if it doesn't and you will promise me to behave like a friend, then I shall be glad to hear from you again soon. Yours truly, Greta.'[4] A few months later, what was to become Garbo's most-quoted catchphrase almost creeps into the correspondence. 'Whenever I am left to myself, I long so dreadfully for the theatre, for, after all, Eva, there's everything I want there.' 'Whenever I'm left to myself,' she writes; not quite 'I want to be alone,' but accepting, if not relishing, the prospect. One story has it that Greta was a stage-struck fan of Carl Brisson, the Danish boxer turned matinée idol, and was once serenaded by him in song while a spotlight isolated her. If true, it makes a bizarre contrast with the white-faced, fleeing woman who looked like the plague-victim of contaminating publicity.

Something more in character occurred between the summer of 1920 and mid-1921. Except for the fact that it was a nervous illness, requiring several weeks in the country to recuperate, we can only guess at its nature. Maybe Greta's anaemia, the counterpoint of an over-stimulated imagination, got the upper hand. In later years, Garbo was never thrilled by anything until it happened, and sometimes not even then. It hurt too much if expectation outran event. In the film industry, where most things that are anticipated do not happen or do not come to pass in the way they are anticipated, circumstances as well as temperament would reinforce such an outlook. A letter to a close friend has a trace of melancholia. 'To be quite honest, I haven't thought of you, for the simple reason that I don't think of anything. I have become pretty indifferent to everything.'

Not quite true. On 26 July 1920, Greta had begun work as a trainee in the millinery department of the Paul U. Bergstrom department store in Stockholm. The six-day-week job paid about $35 – a respectable enough wage for a shopgirl in those days. And after a few months, early in 1921, she had faced a camera professionally for the first time, modelling hats of felt and straw for the store's spring catalogue. Her first chance to act for a movie camera came soon afterwards in an advertising short made for the store by Captain Ragnar Ring, a director of cinema commercials, who chose her for a 'How Not to Wear Clothes' comedy. She modelled ludicrous bits of apparel, sending herself up with the sort of good-natured tomfoolery people nowadays reserve for their home movies. A few months later, compliant to Ring's direction again, she made comedy out of gluttony as a girl in a bakery advertisement ingesting cream cakes at the tea-table with the rapaciousness of a woman just liberated from a rigorous diet. She looks a woman, too, pounds heavier and some years older than her fifteen years, with a face plump enough to dimple into animated smiles between mouthfuls.

Part of the film is set in the Strand Hotel's roof garden and as Garbo takes a mincing sip at her coffee-cup the camera cuts to one of Sweden's best-known young actors

eating next to her apparently by accident. He is Lars Hanson. A few years later Garbo would be co-starring with him in Sweden, then in America. The camera does not show the Royal Dramatic Theatre, which is only a few hundred yards away, opposite the hotel, across the Nybroviken inlet in Stockholm's waterfront: even sooner, Garbo would be a student there.

From now on, the timeliness of Garbo's encounters takes on a fatefulness that is not simply the product of romantic hindsight. Had she not been moved from the millinery to the dress department when Erik Petschler, the producer-director of some fairly low-brow comedies, came in to buy clothes for his new film, she would possibly never have met the actresses he had in tow and been encouraged by them, after she had shyly spoken of her own 'début' in the movies, to audition for Petschler the next day during her lunch hour. He accepted her, more for her well-rounded figure than her touching but irrelevant recitation of a classroom poem. She left her job almost at once, giving as her reason, 'To enter the films.' Words of a determined romantic.

Peter the Tramp (*Luffar-Petter* in Swedish) is Garbo's

OPPOSITE, TOP The first chance to appear professionally before a camera, modelling millinery.

OPPOSITE, BOTTOM 'Hats for Ladies and Girls': under all of them, Greta Gustafsson. The PUB department store catalogue, spring 1921.

ABOVE Behind the cake plate, a surprisingly mature (and plump) sixteen-year-old in the advertising short shot on the Strand Hotel's roof-garden.

RIGHT Cheerfully sending herself up in the 'How Not to Wear Clothes' screen commercial.

feature début. Written, produced and directed by Petschler, and starring him in the dual role of tramp and small-town dandy, it uses Garbo as a bathing belle who might have come from a Mack Sennett slapstick troupe. She has not much to exhibit except her plump figure, doing calisthenics in satin gym shorts to the despair of a humourless instructress, or creating a riper appearance in a thigh-length swimsuit at the lake-side. Petschler said later, 'She had ambition.' It is all that can be said, or needs to be, though it gained her a few sardonic lines in a magazine, *Swing*, which noticed the movie at its première the day after Christmas, 1922, and captioned the newcomer's picture: 'Greta Gustafsson. May perhaps become a Swedish film star. The reason: her Anglo-Saxon appearance.'

The snide remark did not quench Greta's ambition: neither did it bring more offers of movie work, though she appeared as an uncredited, even unidentifiable 'extra' in at least one other film. It was Petschler who told her she needed training; and exactly a year after she had left her salesgirl's job, she applied to audition for one of the twelve or fewer places which offered free tuition at the Academy of the Royal Dramatic Theatre. It was already July. The jury heard aspirants in August. Had Garbo missed the auditions, she would have had to wait another year, and her life and career might have been very different. A friend of Petschler's, a drama coach, turned her over to his daughter for some rapid cramming. Signe Enwall coached her in two of the Academy's set pieces from plays by Ibsen and Selma Lagerlöf; in one she was a strong-willed woman, in the other a shy girl. She also chose an excerpt from Victorien Sardou's play *Madame Sans-Gêne*. Accounts differ on this – as on so many crucial moments in Garbo's career. But all her previous acting experience had been in vigorously comic roles: she seemed to have a natural talent for comic effects. John Bainbridge quotes Signe Enwall as saying, 'The fact that her knowledge of the drama wasn't wide didn't matter. What really counts in an actress is contact with real, everyday life and an ability to feel and understand it. In that sense [she] was probably extremely well-equipped. She was very mature for her age.'[5] The role of Sardou's washerwoman who becomes a duchess and reads a gruff lesson in manners to the hoity-toity ladies of Napoleon's court would not have been beyond Garbo's backstreet experience of life. She did the Lagerlöf monologue first for her judges, then the Sardou one. She never got to the Ibsen: the jury felt they had heard enough. Three days later she was told she had been accepted, one of seven.

Even as part of a class at the Academy, Garbo was already displaying some of the idiosyncracies which later set her apart. Shyness, along with the ignorance of a girl who had left school at fourteen, and also her lack of money, combined to distance her from classmates who were more sophisticated or wealthy. Frugality and few possessions, the lot of many hard-up students, later became Garbo's obsessive trademarks. She acquired them out of the necessity of a time when a scholarship pupil was paid only $50 a month, and retained them amidst the luxury of days when she earned tens of thousands of dollars a week. A black velvet cloak was a favourite garment. Wrapped around her by day, it covered a multitude of make-do-and-mend repairs to old frocks; by night, worn to public performances of plays at the Royal Dramatic Theatre, it 'dramatized' her – set her further apart. Circumstances were forming temperament: the dramatic possibilities

inherent in 'alone-ness' were being explored, tasted and possibly liked. Garbo modelled some clothes, appeared in an advertisement for a Lancia car, and, according to one of her few close friends, Mimi Pollak, kept guardedly silent in her fellow-students' company till she had gained confidence, which she then maintained through compulsive independence. Asking hardly anyone back to her impoverished home, she liked to 'materialize' like someone with no background – the way that most of the vamps she played in her early movies often did with hazardous and heartbreaking effects. It is remembered by some that she also took to coming in late, appearing when the rest of the students were having their coffee-break. The Academy was a highly disciplined place: punctiliousness and punctuality were drilled into the students and behaviour like Garbo's demonstrated her independence although not, as yet,

ABOVE Summer of '22: her first character role, as a sturdy bathing belle (in front) in Erik Petschler's *Peter the Tramp*. A Swedish reviewer called her casting 'a dubious pleasure'.

OPPOSITE Shooting a Mack Sennett-style scene by the lakeside. 'She had ambition,' said the film's director.

the 'insubordination' she was to show Louis B. Mayer.

Garbo did not complete her two-year Academy course: but in the fifteen or so months before films claimed her for good, the kind of teaching she received refined the intuition that enabled her to make such a remarkable impact on the screen. The Academy's teaching was designed to bring students to a pitch by making them use body, mind and instinct: they worked by means of their 'physicality', their awareness of their body, to attain states of being that let them enter imaginatively into character. The thing that strikes one about this method is how closely it resembles The Method – in aims, anyhow, if not in all the complex codifying that Stanislavsky achieved. To read some of Stanislavsky's manuals on the art of acting after seeing a Garbo film is to find the nature of her performance already analysed; which is not to suggest Garbo consciously employed The Method. It was hers by instinct: Academy training only sharpened it.

Her friend and collaborator Mercedes de Acosta said of her many years later: 'Like Duse, in a manner of speaking, she is vibrantly intuitive. Greta was practically never directed in a scene. She would go out on a set and, knowing the character, she would simply and completely *become* that character.'[6] Almost every eye-witness report of Garbo on the film set – there were fewer eye-witnesses as her power to exclude them became absolute – stresses the same point: the amazing suddenness with which her nature changed the instant she started acting. Edmund Goulding, who

directed her in the silent version of *Anna Karenina* (retitled *Love*: 1927), observed: 'In the studios she is nervous. Rather like a racehorse at the post – actually trembling, hating onlookers. At the first click of the camera, she starts pouring forth Garbo into the lens.' Those daydreams on the outhouse roof were kindled into physical concentration at the Academy: later on, the film camera would translate them into something even rarer: spiritual, almost tangible feeling. She would finish the day's shooting dead tired: drained of energy, her body felt its weight. One should never forget how self-conscious Garbo was of her body. She had already reached her grown-up size when she was a mere twelve. 'Everywhere I went as a child, I was pointed at because I was so big for my age – so very big.' Perhaps this was a bond of sympathy when Mauritz Stiller, himself well above average in height even by Scandinavian standards, found this large-limbed woman walking into

OPPOSITE, TOP Garbo (left) with an unidentified friend (centre) and her elder sister Alva whose own career as film actress ended abruptly and tragically with her death from tuberculosis in 1926.

OPPOSITE, BOTTOM With classmates at the Royal Dramatic Theatre Academy, 1923: (from left) Mona Martenson, Arnold Sjöstrand, Barbro Sjöstrand, Tore Lindwall, Vera Schmiterlöw, Georg Funkquist, Alf Sjöberg, Lena Cedarström, Carl-Magnus Thulstrop, Laurin, Mimi Pollak and Greta.

RIGHT Earning pin money as a part-time model while at drama school.

BELOW With classmate Vera Schmiterlöw, advertising the latest Lancia model.

his office for a part he was casting in his new film. It was the fatal meeting.

Certainly, it was not the first time the two had met. Any filmmaker as successful and ostentatiously gregarious as Stiller was in Stockholm, with the gift of small parts in his pocket, would have been bound to attract the Academy students. Garbo already had an introduction to him from Erik Petschler: but it was perhaps lucky for her that she had not too much screen experience behind her. For the man who was to shape the screen Garbo more thoroughly than any other force outside herself, preferred working with players who were inexperienced, even naïve. He held film acting to be a question of 'feeling' a role – sometimes the gifted amateur could do it more effectively than the trained professional. In this, Stiller was remarkably like another star-maker, the autocratic Elinor Glyn, even then practising her gift of 'divination' on behalf of Hollywood studio chiefs who credited this enormously popular self-publicist and author of 'scandalous' Edwardian novels like *Three Weeks* with talismanic qualifications for sensing which players could project romantic love on the screen. Rudolph Valentino was one of her choices; so was Clara Bow, for whom she devised the 'It Girl' description. Stiller, like Mme. Glyn, knew that the eyes were central to film acting: the player who could return the camera's look with a feeling that was not measurable by any focus-puller, he or she was the rarest of finds.

Garbo has related that he looked her straight and long in the eyes, like a camera. She was awkward and nervous: characteristically, he had kept her waiting, a tactic he used a lot in business deals to show his independence. Garbo had put on her lowest-heeled shoes, to make herself look more petite. Stiller seemed gruffly out of patience with her awkwardness; he told her to take off her hat and coat as if she had not heard him order her to do so the first time. He looked her over, then cursorily asked for her telephone number. Garbo said later, ' "He isn't interested," I thought. When they're not interested, they always ask your telephone number. So I put on my hat and coat and went out.' Stiller, however, did promise to call her to the studios for a screen test; and after she had gone, he told his associates, 'There is something extraordinary about this one. I must see what it is.'

When Garbo arrived for her test, Stiller once again kept her waiting a couple of hours, to increase her nervousness and so, he felt, make her more amenable to direction. He then asked her to feign illness for him. Did he detect the way that Garbo's tired look on occasions of strain and stress could be turned by a camera into an impression of love-hungry passion? She lay down on a divan and registered nothing but timidity. 'Act, Miss Gustafsson, act!' Stiller commanded. 'Have you never been inside a drama school?' It was Garbo's movements, especially as she walked around the set while Julius Jaenzon, the cameraman, photographed her in medium and long-shot, which impressed Stiller. The movements and the face – 'You get a face like that in front of a camera only once in a century,' he told executives at Svensk Filmindustri – made him offer Garbo her first major role. Her *feelings*: these were things *he* could supply.

To understand the marriage of talents that was about to be contracted, one has to understand Mauritz Stiller. He was twenty-two years older than Garbo, just turning forty, that is. He had been born Mowscha Katzmann, in Helsinki's Jewish ghetto; and by the political geography of the time, that made him a subject of the Czar. His mother had killed herself, his father died when he was still a child; Mowscha was reared, in the Semitic custom of charity to one's own race, by a family friend, a cap-maker. Having rich, decorative and costly materials within his reach, if not his means, gave the youthful Stiller an early, irrepressible liking for the opulent, man-of-the-world exterior and the sophisticated poses that went with it. He was a dandy, narcissist and fantasist: probably he was also homosexual. Having to learn survival quickly, he developed a cunning indistinguishable from self-confidence. He had a Jewish instinct for deal-making, a capacity to arrange affairs to his own best advantage, with all the tactics that could be enlisted to that end. Vanity, ambition, a showy disposition, a talent for seducing or bullying people into doing what he wanted, and an often self-deluding confidence to pretend he had the means to carry out his promises and then intrigue for ways to acquire them: with such characteristics, Mauritz Stiller ought to have been an immediate success in Hollywood. Unfortunately, while he had failings that actually buttressed his position in the small but artistically flourishing Swedish film world, the same were to prove fatal for his career in the highly-geared Hollywood film factories. He had an incorrigible stubbornness, a tendency to overreach himself, and an arrogance that invited retribution from anyone with the means and disposition to make life difficult for him.

Stiller probably came to Sweden from Finland as a refugee from conscription, when Russia and her satellite were sending troops into the disputed Port Arthur area in 1905. He swiftly found himself a 'protectress' in a Swedish opera star; but failing as a stage actor in several minor companies, he drifted into film work. In that make-believe art, where reality could be re-modelled to the creator's will and vision, Stiller found his metier. Between 1911 and 1923, when he tested Garbo for a role in *Gösta Berlings Saga*, he had turned out nearly forty films, from two-reel melodramas to adaptations of literary or stage works, some of which had added to the Swedish cinema's reputation for exploring the subtleties of human conduct with sophistication and psychological realism. Stiller's 1920 comedy *Erotikon* made witty use of postwar emancipation in social and sexual manners – rather as Cecil B. DeMille's marital comedies with Gloria Swanson were doing in America – by showing a rebellious young wife eloping with a sculptor while her husband in his turn elopes with his niece.

The leading female character in *Erotikon* exercised a fascination on Stiller. By nature, he preferred women who entered his mind rather than his bed. Where a feminine nature was laminated to a masculine will, women were more than escorts for his vanity: they completed his idealized picture of himself. He liked to have power over them. He was continually criticizing other people, altering the way they looked, dressed, spoke, moved, so that they matched an ideal by which aspects of himself could be artistically transformed and accommodated. He was mentally seduced by the heroine of *Erotikon*. Devise another plot like it, he commanded the film's scenarist

The famous name becomes official. On 9 November 1923, Greta's mother 'respectfully requests permission' for her daughter to assume the surname 'Garbo'.

Till överståthållareämbetet.

Undertecknad får härmed vördsamt anhålla om tillstånd
för min omyndiga dotter fröken Greta Gustafsson att få
antaga släktnamnet Garbo
Prästbevis bifogas.
Stockholm den 9 november 1923.
Anna Gustafson.
Bevittnas:
Monica Mårtensson   Ragnar Solf

Min moders förestående ansökan biträdes av mig.
Stockholm den 9 november 1923.
Greta Gustafsson.
Bevittnas:
Monica Mårtensson   Ragnar Solf

Arthur Norden. Then, according to one version, he added, 'But first we must get a name for the woman in it, one that's modern, elegant, international' – like Mauritz Stiller's reputation – 'that means the same and says just as clearly who she is in London and Paris as in Budapest and New York' – the film director's ideal state. Norden, a history specialist, turned for inspiration to the exotic patronym of Bethlen Gabor, Hungary's seventeenth-century king, and Stiller rolled it round his tongue appreciatively. He and Garbo were very sensitive to the *sound* of words, their imaginative stresses as much as their vocal ones. Mercedes de Acosta remembers mentioning a Russian word, 'toscar', to Garbo 'who repeated it many times, pronouncing it richly and turning it, as it were, round her tongue like someone who might be speaking a beloved name'.[7] Stiller apparently worked the same way, trying accent and spelling variations of Gabor until he lighted on – Garbo.

But inevitably, there are other versions. Mimi Pollak has claimed she helped her friend select a prefix 'Gar-' from registrars' lists at the Ministry of Justice (where she had a friend who would help them avoid a clash with some living person's name), and add a '-bo' from another surname. Stiller liked it; and Garbo said one advantage was that she would not have to change the initials on her personal linen. This seems the likelier story. For one thing, that dour remark emphasizing practicality over make-believe has the ring of the emerging Garbo. Stiller's tale of royal antecedents has the feel of *a posteriori* reasoning: it 'sounded better' to make a royal connection than attribute his star's name to a girlish invention. 'Garbo' is still a pre-eminently rare name in Sweden. There are twenty-one pages of 'Gustafsson' (or its variants) in the 1979 Stockholm telephone directory, but only one 'Gardebo', one 'Garbom', and no Garbo. There is another pointer to the likelihood of this origin. When she got round to registering her formal change of name, from Gustafsson to Garbo, at the Ministry of Justice, on 4 December 1923, one might have expected Mauritz Stiller to be a witness if he had been 'the onlie true begetter'. His name does not appear on the document. A classmate of Garbo's, Mona Martenson, witnessed the change. Greta Gustafsson probably regarded 'Garbo' as a *stage* name – and she used it in plays presented by Academy students in 1924. But by March that year it appeared for the first time on the place where the world was to know it: on the screen, amongst the credits of *Gösta Berlings Saga*.

Playing the part of the young Countess Elizabeth Dohna who falls in love with a defrocked tutor (Lars Hanson) was agony for Garbo. Stiller was a perfectionist to a neurotic degree, and gave her as many pains as he himself took over her deportment, lighting and make-up. Infinitely patient at times, at others he stopped the camera to roar rebukes at her. He was not so much remoulding her figure, which he had deemed on the plump side (the camera could take care

TOP The face of stardom takes shape: Garbo in *Gösta Berlings Saga*.

LEFT With co-star Gerda Lundeqvist, on whom Garbo modelled parts of her own persona. 'So much soul and so tired, always,' she said of her.

OPPOSITE, TOP Location shooting, summer 1923: (from left) photographer Julius Jaenzon; director Mauritz Stiller; lighting technician Barascutti; wigmaker Ramsten; Mona Martenson; Lars Hanson; Garbo.

OPPOSITE, BOTTOM The man, for once, has the upper hand in a romantic scene. With Lars Hanson in *Gösta Berlings Saga*.

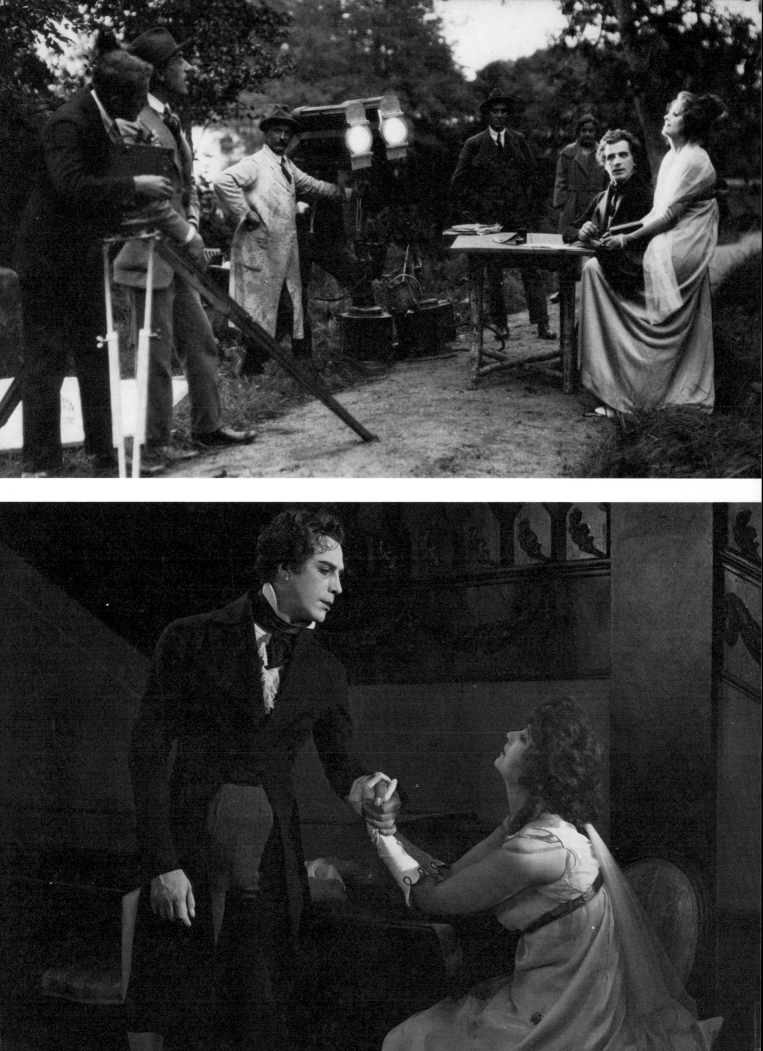

of *that* illusion); he was reconstructing her 'soul', ever nearer his own ideal. To a Swedish journalist who interviewed her during the shooting, Garbo pleaded timidly, 'Please don't write down everything that slips out of my mouth. I am one of those people who don't think – I talk first and think later . . . . Stiller shapes people according to his will . . . . I am one of those nice, ordinary people who suffer terribly if one is mean to them.' Four years later in Hollywood, already powerful enough to banish strangers from the set, the same nervous tone surfaces in an American interview. 'I cannot help [being restless]. That is why I never want people to see me when I am acting . . . . I stay by myself all I can while I am making a picture. I sit in one corner alone or go to my dressing room' – like the child she once described herself as being, 'crawling into a corner and thinking things over'. Outsiders were kept at bay to allow the appearance of the 'insider' – the emotion behind the eyes – of which only the camera was privileged witness.

Gösta Berlings Saga, premièred in two parts, on 10 and 17 March 1924, and running almost four hours, was a popular success, though some critics reacted coolly. They felt Stiller had gutted Selma Lagerlöf's novel for its highlights and turned out an entertainment that was part adventure (a sleigh-ride with wolves in pursuit), part spectacle (a conflagration in a manor house) and part love-story. It is in the last part that Garbo's somnambulistic power reveals for the first time how she could suggest an infinity of emotions even while registering only abstraction. Some of the Swedish reviews betrayed a slight sense of irritation, even bafflement, with her 'still-life acting'. Narrative acting it may not be, but the spiritual interior is the place she inhabits: drifting through a garden picking flowers, gliding with a midnight lamp through the castle, and palpitating with pure emotion (in the first real close-up of her career) as she and Lars Hanson flee from the wolves.

One wonders if any critic saw in Lars Hanson a Stiller-like figure, given to dramatic exaggerations of passion ('I am lord of ten thousand kisses and thirteen thousand love-letters,' the title-card pants at one point) and the pursuit of an idealized love on-screen which had affinities with the director's own Pygmalion-type involvement off-screen. 'She's still inexperienced,' Stiller told his associates. 'But I'm ruthless with her. Wait till I've broken her in.'

For making the film, Garbo was paid $600, then sent back to her class-room at the Academy by Stiller who busied himself re-editing the two parts into one, shorter feature for the German distributors who had paid a handsome $25,000 for the rights. The re-editing apparently emphasized Garbo's role even more. Swedish filmmaking had to be a summer occupation, except when the story called for snow; and Stiller told Garbo not to make any plans for those months. Perhaps he feared that other producer-directors, witnessing his 'find', would have a part in their films for her. He made it a condition of the Berlin première that she attend it, persuading the Germans to pay for their travel and a première gown for Garbo.

As well as tutoring her for the screen, Stiller was inevitably conferring some of his personal attitudes on the shy girl. The pair of them already had physical resemblances: Garbo's largish feet matched Stiller's hefty hands, which he used to keep in his pockets, if he could, when the Press photographers were around him. He disliked the Press. Interviews he avoided: it was not in his interest to reveal his chequered past. When he did talk about it, he fancifully 'improved' it. Garbo gratefully took the hint and tenaciously stuck to it. In one long, three-part interview published in *Photoplay*, in 1928, she succeeds in eliding all reference to her work as a department-store salesgirl and model: she does not even mention *Peter the Tramp*. Again, when he was bargaining with film people, Stiller habitually opened negotiations with a show of uninterest in the proposition. To his *protégée*, this gambit was to become second nature.

One of the companions who travelled with Stiller and Garbo to Berlin for the première of *Gösta Berlings Saga* in September 1924 was the distinguished Swedish actress Gerda Lundeqvist who had played a role in it. This woman deeply impressed Garbo, who, one must suspect, modelled some parts of herself on the Lundeqvist persona. 'She has the most amazing eyes of any person,' Garbo said years later. 'So much soul and so tired, always.' The 'pale and interesting' phlegmatic look coincided nearly enough with her own anaemic condition: that Lundeqvist shared it seemed to give it the stamp of authority. Then again, when Garbo's voice was being heard on the screen in the 1930s, there were some Swedes who believed she had modelled her vocal style on the rather old-fashioned, consciously theatrical tones of Gerda Lundeqvist – though at least one other candidate has been suggested as Garbo's model in the English language, who will be mentioned in her place. The visit also brought out Garbo's extra-sensory relationship with places as well as people. Speaking to the *Photoplay* interviewer, she confessed it was not the sights or sounds of Berlin which gripped and intrigued her, but the *smell* of the city. 'I could feel [sic] the smell long before we were really inside the city – it was as though I had smelt it before . . . been there before.'[8] Over the years the friends she made would find that Garbo, on entering their house or apartment, clasped herself to the walls and smelt the place for its sense of habitation. Good odours meant good omens.

Garbo lived as she worked: with all her senses wide open.

The visit to Germany, whose language she understood at least partially, was Garbo's first 'foreign' trip. It was also her first presentation as 'the star' and the Berlin critics, touched by her world-weariness on the screen and foreshadowing the American reactions to her 'quicksilver movements', gave her a better Press than in Sweden. The film was a sensation: within one week, the distributors got their investment back. Such box-office success was not lost on the Berlin representative of Metro-Goldwyn-Mayer; it is at this stage that America crops up in Stiller's character-istically unformulated plans for his and Garbo's future. But to the suggestion of a Hollywood career, he returned a 'wait and see' answer. He had already completed a co-production deal for his next film between the German distributors, Trianon, who would put up the money, and Svensk Filmindustri, who would contribute film stock and *materiel*. Called *The Odalisque from Smolny*, it was the story of a well-born Russian girl who runs away from a convent in search of her lover and is sold into a Turkish harem before she finds him. The star was to be Garbo.

Had this film been made, Garbo would most likely never have seen Hollywood. Stiller had negotiated a five-year contract for her with Trianon, which suggests he was ready to move out of Swedish production and become a 'European' director. He was being paid nearly $40,000 to make the new film; Garbo was on $100 a week. He set out with his players and crew, ten days before Christmas, 1924, bound for Constantinople and some expen-sive locations. But immersion in the Byzantine society brought out Stiller's weakness for being extravagant with other people's money; soon he was behaving like a Peer Gynt embroiled in film production. Thousands of marks were frittered away on seeking locations – trips that would turn into shopping expeditions – and purchasing 'props' at inflated prices for the interiors that were to be shot back in Berlin. Garbo shared Stiller's high spirits and wore the

Oriental robes he bought for her role in the film at dinner parties and dances. She even turned up at the Swedish Legation and whirled through a boisterous folk-dance in a gown of mandarin scarlet embroidered with Chinese flowers. No wonder she caught the eye of a woman who would exercise great influence on her years later. 'One day in the lobby [of the Pera Palace Hotel],' Mercedes de Acosta recorded in her memoirs, 'I saw one of the most hauntingly beautiful women I have ever beheld.'

Stiller's film was never made. Shortly after Christmas, when the 'present' of more Trianon cash did not mat-erialize, he rushed back to Berlin and found the company bankrupt. 'It was a shock not making that picture,' Garbo admitted. Then she added a remark that throws intriguing light on her relationship with Stiller at this unexpected dip in their fortunes: 'But it was none of my fault. Although I was so restless, why should I have worried? There were other companies and I was young – and was alone in a big wonderful city.' Not for long. Stiller reclaimed her. Prudently he hung on in Berlin. To go back to Stockholm would be too humiliating; besides, he was personally indebted to the film financiers there. He and Garbo stayed in Berlin, lodged in splendour at the Esplanade on their remaining film funds, waiting, Micawber-like, for some-thing to turn up.

Someone soon did. It has been generally assumed that Garbo and Stiller met Louis B. Mayer 'sometime' later in that spring of 1925, and he then and there engaged them for Hollywood. This cannot be the case. The first document in the MGM files is Garbo's 'letter of intent' to become an actress at MGM, and its date-line is Berlin, 30 January 1925. She made up her mind – or had it made up for her – far earlier than generally thought. It looks as if she and Stiller grabbed at Hollywood as an attractive solution to the débâcle they had suffered *before* the German filmmaker, G. W. Pabst, came to their rescue by offering Garbo a part in *Die Freudlose Gasse* (*The Street of Sorrow* in the USA, *The Joyless Street* in England).

'Gentlemen,' Garbo began her letter of intent to MGM, 'In consideration of your providing me with first-class steamer and railroad passage' – Stiller's bargaining hand may be detected in this luxurious perquisite – 'from Berlin to Culver City, USA, I agree to enter into a written contract with you for my services as a motion picture actor ....' It was a five-year contract, beginning at $400 per week and rising, at yearly options to be exercised by MGM, to respectively $600, $750, $1000 and $1250 a week, 'when working'. The contract was to be drawn up after she got to Culver City; and the letter ended, 'It is understood that you are to furnish gratis the clothes required for the films I am to play in.' Thus was Garbo's career clinched. She undertook, further, to leave for America 'not later than 15 April 1925'. It is safe to assume that if Garbo had committed her fortunes to Hollywood by January, Stiller had done so even earlier: he was not a man to let go of his *protégée* at this stage. 'All the business was done with Mr Stiller,' Garbo later recalled. 'Whatever Mr Stiller said, I always knew was the best thing to do. I would say "Is it good?" and if he said "It is good," I would do it.'

Just when the two of them actually came face to face with

A rare photograph of the German première of *Gösta Berlings Saga* in Berlin, September 1924. Garbo is on Stiller's left.

Louis B. Mayer, it has not been possible to establish precisely. Mayer had come to Europe in some haste to sort out the enormous financial catastrophe that shooting *Ben-Hur* in Rome's film studios was becoming. He ordered immediate retreat to Hollywood, and then he pushed on north, into Germany. He had seen *Gösta Berlings Saga* in Hollywood, where Lillian Gish had told him that if he could secure its male star Lars Hanson to play opposite her in *The Scarlet Letter*, then she would put up her stainless reputation as moral collateral for getting the American censors to agree to the filming of this controversial tale of adultery. (For Hanson it would mean going from one defrocked minister to another clerical sinner.) This was not the last favour that Gish unwittingly did Garbo, whom Mayer now met for the first time as he talked to Stiller in Yiddish and German in a suite at the Adlon, to which Stiller had moved from the Esplanade, the better to impress Mayer. 'I guess he looked at me out of the corner of his eye,' Garbo recalled, 'but I did not see him.' She sat there, present but remote, as she had been taught to do at all these film deals. Mayer asked Stiller to come to Hollywood. He had already cabled home to ask another recent Swedish 'import', the director Victor Sjöström, whom MGM had inherited with the merging of the Goldwyn and Metro companies in 1924, whether Stiller was worth buying. Seastrom (as the Americans had anglicized him) at once wired back, 'Yes. Bring him.' Stiller at last agreed on the deal he had promised to 'consider' the previous November and the two men shook hands.

It had been an uneasy encounter for Stiller: Mayer had proved a hard though not ungenerous bargainer. Stiller was promised a starting salary of $1000 per week and 'the same kind of advertising and publicity as Victor Seastrom and others of our first-class directors'. His contract had two option clauses: one for a second year at $1250 a week, plus profit participation in the films and a guaranteed $25,000 per picture against 25 per cent of the net profit. The second option gave him $30,000 a picture, plus 25 per cent. Each picture was to be promoted as 'A Mauritz Stiller Production' and he was to be consulted about the casting. He was also required 'not to become in ill repute with the public of America': a 'morals clause' that had appeared in the contracts of the major studios after the Fatty Arbuckle scandal a few years earlier. (This clause was to have some bearing on Stiller's career at MGM.) Mayer left after casting an eye over Garbo and, the story goes, advising her to diet – American men liked their women to be slimmer. There is no romance in contract-making.

Almost at once, it would seem, Stiller and Garbo began to repent of the deal they had made. Maybe one cause for their hesitation was the unexpected arrival of G. W. Pabst at the Esplanade to ask whether Miss Garbo was at liberty for a part in his picture – that of a young girl trying to relieve her family's impoverishment without sacrificing her own virtue. *The Joyless Street* was a sombrely expressionist study of post-war society in a state of moral exhaustion, rife with pessimism, at the mercy of 'profiteers' and the dealers in flesh and soul. Stiller replied, 'You can have her, if you dare take the risk. But I must warn you that you are tackling a stiff proposition. Beautiful pictures can be made of Greta Garbo, if you know how to make pictures; but she cannot act.' Pabst was undeterred. Stiller then demanded, and got, $4,000 for Garbo's services. At that time, amidst the Weimar Republic's spiralling inflation, this hard-currency contract was dazzling enough to suggest what Garbo might command if she remained in Europe.

Illuminatingly, Stiller's next concern was how Pabst intended photographing Garbo. Agfa was the commonest film stock then in use. Stiller required Pabst to use the costlier and superior Kodak stock for all Garbo's scenes. At the first test, the cameraman Guido Seeber was appalled to discover that Garbo, apparently letting her confidence seep away when Stiller was not nearby and in command, went into a spasm of nervous blinking. Of the 300 feet of film taken of her, 290 were unusable. Means of correcting this was found almost accidentally. In the film, a book had to be shown falling off a table: but it fell so quickly that a camera turning at normal speed hardly registered it. The camera was speeded up and the volume's slow-motion descent recorded. A technician suggested trying this on Garbo. Slow motion enabled them to cut out the nervous trembling of her features and when Pabst at last allowed her to see the tests, her confidence returned. (In later years she was to make it an unbreakable rule never to view her rushes, lest self-consciousness set in.)

Being entrusted to a far more methodical director than Stiller – Pabst shot his film in thirty-four days, Stiller had taken six months – may have annealed the professional ambitions in Garbo which Stiller's possessive vanity had first fired. The German was also more of a 'player's director', patiently involved in helping an intuitive actress like Garbo make emotional discoveries in herself and the role. It meant a most remarkable advance in Garbo's ability to impress her 'presence' mentally on a scene instead of merely performing it physically. No doubt her own nervousness helped in playing a hesitant, frightened, pathetic girl. But when Garbo, her pale face spiritually unsoiled by the vice of the streets, touches the glamorously thick fur coat with which the procuress tempts her, she semaphores by the most delicate signals all the vicarious yearning that the pelts and their mirrored reflections inspire. A Stanislavsky pupil would call this the technique of 'objectification', or relating to objects emotionally. (No accident, perhaps, that in later years Garbo found greatest comfort in inanimate objects and pets, rather than in the people whom she chose for long, obsessive friendships that exacted endless attentions from them.) It scarcely diminishes her power of visual articulation to know that Pabst, at Stiller's wily suggestion, played on her love of sweetmeats by holding them out to her as the camera registered her reactions to the world's grosser temptations.

But working with two directors at the same time, one of them giving her the guidelines, the other a Presence on the sidelines, imposed strains she could not control so well. There was at least one short-lived rift with Stiller, and Garbo's life-long bouts of restlessness and insomnia date from this time. The Berlin experience reinforced another aspect of her: a concern, amidst the big money of film-making, with the small change of housekeeping. When the film had been finished, a Pabst employee bought her a first-class ticket for Stockholm and put her aboard the train. 'Oh, I forgot to pay this bill,' she said, as it was moving off. 'Would you settle it for me?' Opening it, he feared it was for

Garbo, already a svelte and alluring creature, in a portrait taken in Stockholm probably before *The Joyless Street*'s première.

some extravagant article. It was for the mending of her shoes. One dollar.

Garbo was Mauritz Stiller's principal financial support in those weeks in Berlin when he was trying to set up new European film deals involving the German consortium UFA. He had had his own living expenses written into her contract with Pabst. Events were stealthily but measurably reversing their importance to one another.

When Garbo had finished her role, she and Stiller returned to Stockholm and there she had a series of portraits taken by a professional photographer that reveal the svelte, alluring and already mysterious creature she had become in the last year. The portraits made by Arnold Genthe when Garbo got to New York are usually the ones that testify to this: and they are credited with turning the sceptical MGM executives' heads her way when they saw what well-positioned light and shadow could do for the new arrival. But 'all Garbo' is there already in these Scandinavian photographs. One can only conclude they were taken for *The Joyless Street*'s première and then left behind in Berlin, or with Garbo's family as a keepsake against her return.

Stiller saw his business deal near enough success to postpone the date he and Garbo were to leave for America. When they attended the première on 18 May 1925, she was already four weeks past her promised departure date for Hollywood. He was still trying to find grounds for breaking his own agreement. One demand he now made was to have his MGM productions distributed in Europe by Svensk Filmindustri. It was a demand he could have had little hope of seeing granted by the 'hard men' of Hollywood: he may have hoped it would be a deal breaker. But Mayer was

adamant. A week or so after the Berlin première, Stiller received an angry cable from the MGM mogul: 'We have contract with you and expect you to live up to it. There were no conditions that we would lease our pictures to Filmindustri for distribution, as our distributing organization distributes our pictures in accordance with best possible interests for our company and cannot complicate contract with matters connected with Filmindustri. If you have obligations with Filmindustri you must adjust them. You were not afraid to come [to] America when you talked with me, and Seastrom [is] doing very well in America. All these matters are your personal affairs. We cannot change from original proposition. Advise me when you sail. Regards. Loumayer.' Stiller realized he was up against a tough machine called a Hollywood studio. He bowed his long, lantern-jawed head to the inevitable. In any case, Garbo would have to go to Hollywood, and he was not prepared to lose her.

So at the end of June, 1925, accompanied by Stiller who had had his English tailors send him a new suit for the occasion, Garbo took tearful leave of her mother, her brother Sven and sister Alva (whom she was destined never to see alive again) and boarded the boat train for Gothenburg and the voyage to America. 'Mother, I will be back in one year,' she said.

ABOVE Garbo in *The Joyless Street*: her sensuality appears for the first time.

OPPOSITE, TOP Pabst begins Garbo's long affair with mirrors.

OPPOSITE, LEFT With Valesca Gert as the procuress.

OPPOSITE, RIGHT On the programme, Garbo shares the top billing.

Garbo in *Love*, 1927: 'I like to be alone.'

THE MGM YEARS
1925-1941

THE TEN-DAY voyage across the Atlantic on the *Drottningholm* restored some of Stiller's health (he was showing the first symptoms of the elephantiasis that would inflate his already large limbs and strike him down a few years later); but it did nothing to build his confidence. Can he have realized by then that Hollywood's production system might well force him and Garbo to work apart? That their 'ideal union', as he characterized it to friends, might be broken by 'supervisors' who, at MGM anyhow, were unsympathetic to Pygmalions and Galateas?

What hit him and Garbo as they disembarked on 6 July 1925 was the absence of a welcoming committee, and the presence of one of New York City's fiercest heat waves. They gamely posed by the liner's rail, Garbo arching her figure, as she had been taught, to give a slim-line effect to hips that were broad when viewed from the front. Their modish Continental clothes were as ill-fitted for the sweltering weather of an alien city as the wearers. For the first time, their language cut them off from the people around them, and this isolation made them feel friendless. The MGM office, apparently un-briefed about the new contract couple, mustered its slender vacation resources and sent a junior employee, Swedish-speaking Hubert Voight, hurrying to extend a makeshift greeting with a freelance photographer, Jimmy Sileo, who performed the chore (for a flat fee of $25) of snapping Greta Garbo standing for the first time on American soil.

Their next few weeks were aimless and frustrating. Maybe by company policy, Stiller was being cut down to size; his characteristically late-in-the-day demand for the Swedish company to distribute MGM's films had alerted all Mayer's mistrustful instincts. Cooling his heels might cool his head. Keeping cool was, in fact, largely what he and Garbo did. She passed hours at the Commodore Hotel soaking in cold tubs while outside the temperatures sizzled in the upper 80s. He kept running into the language barrier and scarcely less resistant executives at MGM's offices on Broadway when he tried putting calls through to Mayer on the Coast. He claimed Mayer had promised to pay their New York living expenses for a fortnight. It took weeks to sort this out. Almost as long was spent urging the MGM officials to make a screen test for Garbo; and when one was grudgingly made, it was obvious to Stiller that the photographer did not know how to light her. Stiller demanded they make another test. He was turned down flat and called an interfering nuisance. 'Everything is in a mess,' said Garbo.

When Stiller had seen he could make no headway on his distribution demands, he had accepted fate and signed his MGM contract on 9 July 1925; he was due to begin work in Hollywood on 12 September, when his pay would start. But he refused to make a move until Garbo's interests had been taken care of. The MGM lawyers found they were dealing with a two-headed monster. Stiller demanded that her starting salary be doubled, and her contract shortened from a proposed five years to a maximum of three to bring it into line with his own tenure. They stuck their heels in on the money demand, gave way on the length of service – after all, time was not money when yearly options could quickly terminate the arrangement – and thus created, unwittingly, the first great Garbo–Mayer impasse of a few months later.

Efficiency does not appear to have been working at full blast that hot summer in the Broadway office. Though

Garbo finally signed her three-year contract with MGM in New York on 26 August 1925, the document mistakenly referred to the signing taking place in Los Angeles. Far more vigilant eyes in Culver City spotted this a month later. Would it affect the validity? Maybe not, was the legal opinion. But utter consternation ensued on the discovery that Garbo had been under twenty-one years of age when she had signed (she looked considerably older). Incredibly, no one in MGM had thought to check her age! The studio's legal department urgently demanded that Garbo 'ratify' the New York-made contract on arrival at Culver City, 'with her mother's approval'. The lawyer's memo added, '... provided she will do it without quibbling'. In such legal asides one senses the temperamental difficulties in the making. But when she complied with their request and re-signed the deed on 18 September 1925, everyone breathed again.

The one piece of good luck their disorienting sojourn in New York brought Stiller and Garbo turned out to be the studio photographs of Garbo taken by Arnold Genthe, whom they had met through a chance acquaintance. The Vienna-born photographer emphasized the sensuousness of her just-parted lips and her heavy eyelids, the broad smooth brow and the soft mass of hair fanning out like a crown. Provocativeness and spirituality were present in the same persona – and, in Genthe's array of pictures, there seemed not *one* woman, but half a dozen. When some of these were sent to Culver City, they caused enough of a stir to make the executives want the subject present and ready for work. (A persistent story is that when Genthe's favourite study of Garbo appeared in *Vanity Fair*'s November issue, captioned 'A New Star from the North – Greta Garbo', studio talent scouts rushed to find out who and where this divine woman was so as to offer her a contract. If true, it is unlikely this occurred at the meticulously managed MGM studios; but 'not knowing what they'd got' is one of the constant ironies of Hollywood stardom. A sadder and verifiable fact is that when Mauritz Stiller died, he was holding the Genthe picture of Garbo.)

The MGM accounts department shows that nothing was left to chance. Even the petty cash of imminent stardom was checked twice over. The sea journey to America for Stiller and Garbo cost $1463.11. The services while in New York of one Kay Kynt (possibly an interpreter/translator) were charged at $100, half to Stiller, half to Garbo. The bill for the five-day train journey to Culver City – along with a 'secretary', Olaf Rolf, whom Stiller somewhat mysteriously acquired in New York – was $976.95. 'We paid for a compartment each for Stiller and Garbo,' MGM accounts executive Charles Green punctiliously noted, 'and a lower berth for secretary. Supplying two compartments compelled purchasing three tickets instead of two. I deemed it advisable, considering their importance and the length of the journey.' None the less, the cost was charged two-thirds to Stiller, one-third to

TOP LEFT With Stiller in New York on arrival from Sweden. The early pictures show the 'star' postures she soon abandoned when she did not need them.

TOP RIGHT One of the Arnold Genthe portraits, made in August 1925, which alerted MGM executives to 'the Garbo quality'.

LEFT Welcome to Los Angeles. The Swedish-American film colony turns out to greet Stiller and Garbo in what is more like a wedding party than a reception committee.

Garbo. All this should have served as a warning to Stiller. Thrift was the rule at MGM. The extravagant entrepreneurial gesture (at someone else's expense) was severely discouraged.

There was a gratifyingly larger group of welcomers on the platform at Los Angeles. Studio officials were outnumbered by Swedish or Danish friends. In their smart West Coast summer finery flanking Garbo and Stiller, who had been presented with bouquets by children in Scandinavian costume, they look more like a wedding party. Inches above everyone else, with tired eyes despite a smile-for-the-camera look, Stiller stands beside a Garbo who glances shyly away. What were her immediate plans, she was asked; through an interpreter, she replied (to the distress of MGM's publicity department), 'To find a room with a nice private family.' Her attention was caught by the small parcels some of the welcoming committee carried. 'Are they presents for me?' she asked the 'secretary' Olaf Rolf. He replied, 'Kind of.' (Rolf, having reached Los Angeles, now disappears from the story as suddenly as he had entered it.) Then everyone adjourned to a downtown hotel, where the new arrivals freshened up and the 'presents' were opened. They turned out to be bottles of liquor hidden by plain wrappings from the enforcement agents of Prohibition.

The studio rented a beach bungalow for Stiller at Santa Monica and rooms for Garbo at the nearby Miramar Hotel which was managed by a Norwegian who brought homely (and intelligible) accents within earshot. A large number of Hollywood's Swedish colony preferred to cling to the damper coastal regions; though the grey Pacific hardly compensated for Stockholm's sparkling archipelago, homesickness was alleviated by being shared. Snapshots of

LEFT Cold-weather fashion amongst the California palms.

BELOW Garbo and Stiller mark time at Santa Monica, flanked by their compatriots Lars Hanson and Karin Molander.

OPPOSITE 'Oh, how I hate this eternal sun,' she wrote home. Even going barefoot on the beach hardly made it tolerable.

this period have a deceptively tranquil character, as Stiller and Garbo laze on the beach, his big legs tucked awkwardly under him giving him the appearance of a collapsed and clownish marionette, while she looks coolly out from under the new, softer-styled coiffure that the studio had created for her. They were also straightening and capping her teeth and advising her on diet: the remaking of Garbo in the Hollywood image had begun. Inwardly, both were miserable. To be aliens was bad enough; to be inactive was worse. No work had been offered to either. Françoise Rosay, wife of the Belgian director Jacques Feyder who was to come to Hollywood a few years later, has noted in her memoirs that it was deliberate policy on the studios' part to leave even their expensive 'imports' at a loose end for some weeks after arrival. They needed to re-adjust themselves to the faster tempo of a 'company town'. But Stiller was impatient – and he had made a bad beginning with Irving Thalberg, the studio's production chief, a man sixteen years his junior. Thalberg's undersized physique accentuated the discomfiture and irritation he felt in the presence of this loud-voiced Swedish giant.

The publicists were working on Garbo's new image with no great inventiveness. They had decided she was the sporty, outdoor girl, American-style, and were picturing her cuddling lion cubs whilst leaning somewhat apprehensively away from the full-grown mother, posing with beefy athletes from the University of Southern California, or 'on

her mark' at the sprinting tracks. (Some years later David Selznick, concerned about the publicity treatment being meted out to his discovery, Ingrid Bergman, wrote a memo warning that the way Garbo was handled caused her 'to lose all faith and confidence, and properly so, in the judgment and taste of the publicity department'.[9]) Garbo had a typical Swedish shyness about revealing her personal side in public. One reason she admired Lillian Gish was that 'she is a star who doesn't have to shake hands with boxers'. In fact, Gish was the first Hollywood influence that Garbo found remotely sympathetic. She admired her firm attitude to her employers, her refusal to accept anything second-rate. When Gish fell from grace at MGM a few years later, it was as if she had passed on these qualities to Garbo. Garbo used to be left by Stiller to sit on the set of Gish's film *The Scarlet Letter* while he besieged Thalberg's office demanding a film to direct. Seastrom was directing Gish's

OPPOSITE, TOP A publicity still, 1925, emphasizing the Nordic virtues a baffled studio Press department hoped to find in her.

OPPOSITE, BOTTOM The rituals of star-making, such as being tagged an 'outdoor girl' and checked for muscularity by the University of Southern California athletics coach, gave Garbo an early antipathy to publicity.

BELOW A candid camera shot on the set of her first MGM film *The Torrent*.

RIGHT Garbo pays an admiring visit to Lillian Gish, with her director Victor Seastrom, on the set of *The Wind*.

picture, Lars Hanson was her co-star; just watching her countrymen gave Garbo some solace.

Fate gave her something more valuable at this juncture. For her D. W. Griffith film *Hearts of the World*, made in 1918, Gish had discovered a Dutch photographer, Hendrik Sartov, a genius with soft-focus effects. Sartov became her favourite photographer. Now he got the nod from the American star to undertake the screen test of Garbo which a wearied Thalberg eventually authorized Stiller to make. It was this test that ignited the enthusiasm of another MGM contract director, Monta Bell, who saw it almost by accident while vetting some newsreel material on flood disasters for his planned production of *The Torrent*. Immediately he asked for Garbo. She hesitated. Stiller insisted. Though he was not to direct her, as both had hoped, she had the chance of co-starring with Ricardo Cortez, at that time Rudolph Valentino's rival as a Latin Lover and very soon his posthumous successor. 'It's an important advance,' Stiller counselled.

It was, even though *The Torrent* is otherwise a lamentably lustreless picture. Based on Blasco-Ibanez's best-selling novelette about a peasant girl who becomes a *prima donna*, titillating and sanctimonious by turns, it could never have been a work of art. Its practical function was to serve as a show-case for a Garbo whose personality and appearance are constantly switched around as time and fate transform the heroine's fortunes. She is in rough and ready succession a maudlin sweetheart, a scornful vamp, a jealous inamorata, a great singer graciously condescending to a humble cabaret artist, a woman of the world cynically toting a cigarette holder as she hobnobs with crowned heads, and finally a lonely, fatalistic beauty wedded to no man but only to her vocation. (Sometimes the film gives us an eerie feeling of watching all Garbo's future film roles foretold in one movie.) With each new manifestation, the photography is subtly altered, as if the cameraman were shuffling her cards of identity.

He was. This was the start of her relationship for fourteen years and in nineteen of her films with William Daniels. Daniels was in awe of no star: many were in his debt, as his inward eye assembled and re-assembled their outward images. But like many of Hollywood's pioneers, he was an uncomplicated genius. He was a direct man, refreshingly down-to-earth. Over the years he established a rapport with Garbo possibly closer – certainly more enduring – than that of any single director who worked with her. She was a part of his affections, as well as his professionalism. On lazy Sundays, he would pilot his amateur's biplane over whichever house she happened to have settled in, and wag his wings in friendly salute.

Daniels and she were soon swapping English phrases. Hearing her repeat a lesson to herself, murmuring 'Garbo important', Daniels joined in with, 'Of course, you're important – the most important person on the set.' (Both of them disliked the cocksure Cortez whom Garbo called 'a pumpkin'.) She considered this a second, then continued, 'Yes, Garbo important . . . sardines important . . . .' *Important* or *imported*: it was the same thing when the reviewers of *The Torrent* reacted to the vivid sense of 'foreign-ness' she brought to the screen. The fact that they had seen no American actress like her is not contradicted by notices that compare her to half-a-dozen Hollywood stars like Carol Dempster, Norma Talmadge, ZaSu Pitts or Gloria Swanson, as the critic Richard Watts Jr. did in the

Herald Tribune. 'This does not mean she lacks a manner of her own, however,' he added. Laurence Hall, in *Motion Pictures*, echoed this: 'She suggests a composite picture of a dozen of our best-known stars.' Now it is a sure sign that a new type of film star has arrived when the reviewers are forced to compare her with the old. That is what was happening here among critics who were excited, but groping for the apposite words. That such a comparison is made at all is evidence of a newcomer's impact; a little later will come proof of her individuality, then of her uniqueness. The phenomenon of Garbo's début is that she did not have to wait: all three stages seemed telescoped into one.

Her self-conscious Swedish compatriots looked for 'artistry' in Monta Bell's disjointed film and prophesied the end of Garbo's career when they discerned none; Stiller flew into a violent rage when he saw 'what they had done' to her. But the Swedes, if good critics, were poor prophets: what they overlooked was the impact of her 'personality'. First, there was the surprise of seeing a Scandinavian

OPPOSITE, TOP LEFT No room for interpretation: Monta Bell shows Garbo how he wants it done for a seduction scene in *The Torrent*.

OPPOSITE, TOP RIGHT Publicity shot, 1926: still seeking a kittenish Garbo.

OPPOSITE, BOTTOM With Ricardo Cortez in *The Torrent*. Henceforth, in love scenes, the man was the passive partner.

BELOW Garbo's authentic persona still eludes photographers making wardrobe studies for *The Torrent*.

beauty register Latin passion so physically, if intermittently. While Garbo's third film, *Flesh and the Devil*, is the one generally credited with the horizontal love scenes that became her erotic trademark, there is a moment of great sensual tension in *The Torrent* which fits Garbo and Cortez together in a supine embrace of jigsaw neatness. Her body and the way she used it also struck the American audiences as excitingly unfamiliar. In motion, she relayed a liberated, animal will as her awkward proportions swung into sensuous adjustment. Quite innocently, she elucidated her own appeal when she wrote home despondently to a friend, 'They don't have a type like me out here, so if I can't learn to act they'll soon tire of me, I expect.'

A number of unintentionally amusing things happened on the set of *The Torrent* due to Garbo's not understanding English very well. They also throw light on how fine a line there was between her increasingly lugubrious attitude to events and the amusement this could cause when it was slightly out of joint with them. (Later on, a whole comedy, *Ninotchka*, would be able to play a series of comic variations on this contradiction.) In one dramatic scene she was directed to sit down at a piano and sing a line or two from the popular song, 'I want to be happy,/But I can't be happy/Till I make you happy, too'. Her mood was supposed to alter as she sang it, from sad to gay. Not comprehending the words, Garbo continued singing 'Ay vont to be 'appy,/But Ay can't be 'appy,' in tones of deepest melancholy, till the entire set could suppress their laughter no longer. She joined in when the joke was explained to her.

Garbo alleges that Louis B. Mayer tried to pressure her into extending her three-year contract into a five-year one within a week or so of starting *The Torrent*. There could be no clearer indication that MGM now knew the prize they had got – the daily rushes confirmed it – and wanted to hang on to it. Mayer was only being prudent. He could not afford to finance and advertize her films, he told her in a letter, if he was not sure of having her services for longer than three years. A five-year contract, he patiently explained, was related to a movie's commercial life-time. Any hit she made would still be around for two years after Garbo might have gone to another film company. MGM would be left promoting the movie, while its star profited their rivals. But Garbo could never grasp commercial sense if it contradicted her own emotional logic. 'Why do they want me to sign a contract for five years when I haven't even finished my first picture?' Besides, Stiller's was a three-year deal. She wanted to be free to leave when he did.

Eager to capitalize on her sensational début, MGM shelved their contract demands and rushed her into another film, *The Temptress* – to be directed by Stiller. He was elated to be working, Garbo overjoyed to be with him again. For all of ten days they were together; then, abruptly, Stiller was removed from it. Suspicious students of studio politics have interpreted this as a deliberate

TOP 'With her first glance,' wrote a French critic, 'this shy Baltic girl mesmerized the Babbits of America.' Garbo as the *prima donna* in *The Torrent*.

LEFT Interpreter or persuader? Probably both, Sven-Hugo Borg rarely quit Garbo's side on the MGM lot, and later claimed that his influence replaced Mauritz Stiller's.

OPPOSITE In costume for *The Torrent*. Such exotic fashions gave her a lifelong aversion to dressing up.

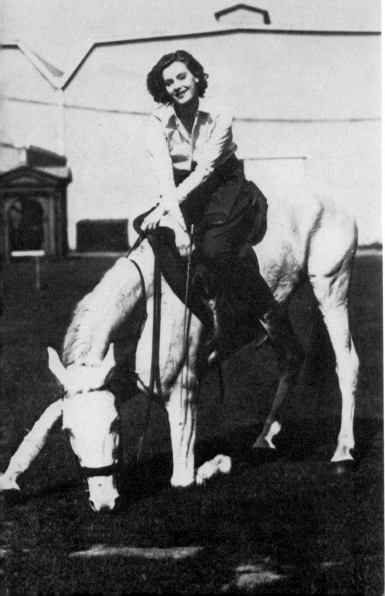

ABOVE For the few days he was in control, Stiller directed some of *The Temptress*'s most spectacular sequences.

LEFT The horse Garbo rode was a 'trick' steed, trained to take direction, too.

OPPOSITE, TOP Stiller, once more the autocrat in command, rehearses Garbo and Antonio Moreno in *The Temptress* in April 1926. A few days after this shot, he was taken off the film.

INSET The celebrated Garbo grip begins to tighten on her man.

OPPOSITE, BOTTOM The stillman on *The Temptress* made this trick shot of Garbo lighting herself and (BELOW) Mauritz Stiller apparently giving himself instructions.

humiliation. The MGM files give no evidence for this. They tend to confirm eyewitness reports that the Swede still had not adjusted to American studio discipline and could neither give direction nor accept directives. Undoubtedly his poor English accounted for his confusing instructions on the set (Seastrom, who had been in America as a boy, never had this trouble). But his occasional incoherence did not abate his arrogance when people stared or stopped work, unable to understand what they were to do. He made it plain, without any difficulty at all, that he thought Antonio Moreno, Garbo's leading man, a vain coxcomb. He ordered him to put his hair up in a pompadour style so as to look taller beside Garbo and wear boots that made her feet look smaller. No male star is so sensitive as one who realizes that the film's favours are being thrown to the lady. Even so, MGM might have worked out a compromise but for one unforgivable sin of Stiller's – he was wasting time and costing money. Hollywood directors blue-printed scenes well in advance of shooting them; Stiller preferred to rehearse them on the spot, letting chance play a creative part in their final form. The system simply was not made for the idiosyncratic artist. Moreover, MGM had recently had a fight with Erich von Stroheim, an extravagant autocrat whose production of *The Merry Widow* was fresh enough in the minds of Mayer and Thalberg to make them vow that another belligerent director, mindless of any interests but his own artistic temperament, would never again attempt to call the tune at their studio.

'When this thing happened to Moje,' Garbo wrote to a Swedish friend, 'I thought the sun would never rise again.' Even worse than Stiller's dismissal was news that had arrived a few days after Stiller started shooting – her sister Alva, a warm, outgoing girl who had been making a film career of her own in Sweden, had died of tuberculosis. The way Stiller handled this event suggests how ruthless he could be in using any means to make Garbo give him the effect he wanted. He held on to the cable for twenty-four hours, then pretended to have it delivered to Garbo on the set, amidst the society carnival that formed the film's opening scenes. An eye-witness called Sven-Hugo Borg, who had been made Garbo's interpreter, recalled: 'The set was hushed in sympathy as the word spread. For a few moments, Garbo sat silent, holding her head in her hands, and then she rose to her feet. "Come, Mauritz, let us go on," she said, and with a smile she took her place on the set.' Did this add the desired shade of desperation to Garbo's features in the sequences directed by Stiller and preserved in the film when Fred Niblo took his place as director?

In the brief period Stiller worked on *The Temptress* he managed to create a magical, completely individual Garbo. His part of the film opens at the fashionable *bal masqué* and abruptly, dramatically, reveals Garbo as an unhappily married woman in a box spurning her latest lover, then

TOP Garbo was an 'interior' actress, at her best in repose: *The Temptress* is the film that confirms this.

RIGHT Revellers at the *bal masqué*, in *The Temptress*'s opening sequence, serenade Garbo at a rehearsal in the sunshine.

OPPOSITE TOP Garbo with Antonio Moreno.

OVERLEAF Posing (one suspects very unwillingly) for a vampish set of publicity photos for *The Temptress* with 'Gay Blades' H. B. Warner (with monocle), Roy D'Arcy and Armand Kaliz (with moustache).

fleeing through the revellers like a white exclamation mark. Her thin, tall, tubular body and business-like legs give her flight a tenseness that increases its provocativeness. Suddenly, she comes to grips with Moreno. And then one is struck by a bizarre feature – the tired, strained look on her white face, over which she wears a white half-mask that looks like a sulky rash. On any other actress, such a look of washed-out weariness would resemble listlessness. On Garbo, though, it has a yearning tautness: it plays dramatically against the desperation of a character whose misfortune it is to have every man she meets fall helplessly, sometimes fatally in love with her while she responds with a hopeless, nymphomaniac compulsion. She seizes Moreno. No tender vine, this; but one with an embrace which suggests that, given time, it will dominate the host plant. It is the earliest appearance of the famous Garbo grip of the woman in love who reaches first. For her, from the start, love was always intense, though not necessarily always a heavyweight passion. She surprises us by planting a sudden, light flurry of kisses, like raindrops, on Moreno's cheek. Blotting out his vision of her with her hand, she places a longer kiss on his lips, then is off – darting phosphorescently through a prismatic scattering of woodland moonlight. The vacuum she leaves is filled with an immense sense of eroticism. 'Garbo', said George Cukor years later, 'had this rapport with an audience. She could let them know she was thinking things, and thinking them uncensored.'[10] *The Temptress* shows us this quality for the first time.

The rest of it, directed by Niblo, shows an immediate coarsening as Garbo is forced into some bad, reach-me-down vamp reactions which suggest that her director practised the same demonstrate-and-imitate techniques he had used on Nita Naldi in *Blood and Sand*, four years earlier. She is pressed into gymnastic reactions, not psychological truths. Never again was she to have such a crude concept forced on her. If MGM got rid of Stiller, at least they retained his vision of Garbo.

She had threatened to walk off the picture when he was taken off it. A dejected Stiller at first encouraged her. Sven-Hugo Borg claims *he* talked her out of it. Borg was employed as her interpreter; but one senses he was also retained as her 'persuader'. 'This, I believe,' he recorded when she returned to the picture, 'was her first act on her own initiative against Stiller's wishes and the end of his influence over her.' The tall, handsome Borg has left a valuable account of the woman whose company he now came to share more and more often in the physical absence of Stiller. Even allowing for some justifiable preening, his insights into her in these early formative days ring true. 'She was tired, terrified and lost' without Stiller. 'As she returned to my side after a trying scene, she sank down

ABOVE With Stiller dismissed from the picture, Garbo suffers stoically the cruder hand of her new director, Fred Niblo (seated).

OPPOSITE *The Temptress* had more than twenty exotic costumes. An impenitent Garbo said, 'I wish they were all bags, and all alike, to jump into quick.'

OVERLEAF Despite *The Temptress*'s lavish wardrobe, Garbo's sex appeal was unconcealable.

beside me and said so low it was almost a whisper, "Borg, I think I shall go home now. It isn't worth it, is it?".' That catch-phrase, shortened into 'I think I go home', soon passed into the repertoire of a legion of Garbo-imitators and helped publicize her strong-willed temperament.

The Temptress also fixed her early dislike of owning a large wardrobe in her private life, for, on-screen, almost every picture she made called for an array of dresses of exotic design. 'More than twenty costumes to try on over and over,' she moaned. 'That is why I do not care about clothes. The *decisions*! There are so many clothes ... I cannot think of them when I am away from a picture.' André Ani, then MGM's chief designer, said, 'She was the despair of the wardrobe department. "Dresses, I wish they were all bags, and all alike, to jump into quick."' Rilla Page Palmborg, the wife of a Swede and a noted journalist, confirmed this impression in one of the earliest American interviews with Garbo – an important one for fixing the image of Garbo, both in her own confused thoughts and in the public's imagination. She appeared 'tall, awkward and self-conscious .... She wore a plain little suit, in need of pressing. Her eyes were shaded with a green visor .... She said that the California sun hurt her eyes.' Garbo confessed that after Stiller's dismissal she had been 'frantic', but further comment was refused. Mrs Palmborg concluded, 'Greta Garbo will fascinate people, but I wager she will always remain more or less a mystery.' As if to tie on the label that certified Garbo's increasingly elusive appeal, the article was headed 'The Mysterious Stranger'.

Stiller's and Garbo's positions were indeed reversed now: he turned morose, listless and pessimistic, the very qualities innate in Garbo. She on the other hand was rushed into a new film a few days after shooting ended on *The Temptress*, which had taken an incredible eighteen weeks to finish in a studio where the average schedule was nearer five. The studio now began to protect one of its investments and loosen the ties that bound it to the other. Garbo had originally been admitted to America on a six-month work permit. In January 1926, MGM applied for another six months – but in July of that year, they requested a year's stay for her, the maximum permitted to a non-resident alien. As for Stiller, a letter to MGM from Loeb, Walker, Loeb, a Los Angeles law firm that represented the studio, advised in May 1926, that 'we do not think you should apply for an extension for Stiller unless you are prepared to use his services after July 6, 1926' – when he would have been a year in America. Stiller lingered in disgrace and frustration. He was obliged to waive screen credit for *The Temptress* to allow Fred Niblo solo billing. Mayer additionally ordered that Stiller's salary plus a 25 per cent surcharge, from the start of his employment at the studio until he began work afresh, should be charged to *The Temptress*. Stiller was not galvanized out of his dejection until Erich Pommer, the German producer then at Paramount, asked that studio's production chief, Jesse Lasky, to try to borrow Stiller from MGM as director of Pola Negri's new film *Hotel Imperial*. Even then, MGM did not exert themselves to get Stiller's work permit extended for the requisite six months until he had actually signed with Lasky. If he was to stay in America, they wished to be sure he was working away from *their* studio, away from Garbo. There is a tantalizing memo dated 12 July 1926 – three days after Stiller's extension had come through – from William A. Orr, of MGM's New York office, to Louis B. Mayer which begins, 'I think I should tell you there was something back of this Stiller case. I mean by that that the Department of Labor had heard something antagonistic to Stiller. I was not able to find out what it was, and I can only assume that it was possibly an anonymous letter sent to the Department by someone who wanted to see him out of the country. You understand, of course, that I have no evidence to go on in voicing this suspicion, but I am convinced there is something working against me on this Stiller matter and I presume if you should want another six months' extension for him, I should find the same or increased antagonism.' Now such discretion in the description 'something antagonistic', and in the reference to an 'anonymous letter', is unusual in a memo of a confidential nature: it tends to be used if morals, particularly sexual ones, come into the reckoning. Hollywood was extremely sensitive to charges of 'moral turpitude' at this date: the Hays Office, its own self-censoring board, was making difficulties for scripts with unconventional scenes, themes or characters, and the fear of Federal censorship was never far off. Even a suspicion that Stiller might prove a public embarrassment must have increased the reluctance to retain his services, whether or not Orr was correct in his assumption. In one assumption he certainly was correct: 'I am assuming that Garbo is one whom you will want to keep as long as possible,' he added.

They did: but they were wary. When Garbo had received the *Flesh and the Devil* script, she went to Mayer. 'I said, "Mister Mayer, I am dead tired. I am sick. I cannot do another picture right away. And I am unhappy about this picture."' She said she could not see any sense in dressing up and continually tempting men in pictures. 'And they said, "That's just too bad. Go on and try on your clothes and get ready."' When she attempted, at Stiller's urging, to select a wardrobe of her own in a less vampish style, Mayer was swift with the rebuke and warning of contractual 'suspensions'. Garbo obeyed instructions – and thus met John Gilbert.

John Gilbert was then Hollywood's most romantic idol and probably its highest-paid male star. The Great Lover patent held by Rudolph Valentino – who was to die two weeks to the day after *Flesh and the Devil* started shooting on 9 August 1926 – was inherited by Gilbert. He was worthy of the succession. He was then twenty-nine – eight years older than Garbo – and had two marriages behind him. He was also an incurable, compulsive romantic, in life as well as art. 'Whatever role he was playing,' said King Vidor who directed him as the gallant Doughboy in his greatest hit, *The Big Parade*, 'he literally contrived to live it off screen.' Romance was like alcohol to Gilbert: it gave him a feeling of being on a permanent, exhilarating 'high'. In 'ordinary' people, this would have been judged an unstable character trait; in a film star, it was a means of projection and protection.

OPPOSITE At a lonely moment in her career, separated from her mentor Mauritz Stiller, Garbo meets the screen's Great Lover – John Gilbert. Off-screen, too, their love affair is beginning. On the set of *Flesh and the Devil*.

OVERLEAF A love sequence from *Flesh and the Devil*.

1 The lovers meet in her husband's absence

2 The husband makes his return

5 Garbo: 'One more day, Leo . . .

6 *How can I let you go?'*

9 Gilbert: 'Forget you?'

10 *. . . Not while I live . . . not if I die.'*

4

8 Garbo: 'So that I may not forget you . . .'

For Garbo, this encounter with an authenticated Great Lover could not have been more timely or influential. His very certainty of who he was, his dedication to living up to what he represented, had a steadying effect on Garbo at this lonely moment in her career when her mentor was being forced to seek work away from her and no satisfaction was to be gained from either the salary she was being paid or the range of roles she was being offered. Moreover, Gilbert was really the first American she had met. The Americans she had observed in New York, during the anxious, depressing weeks when she and Stiller waited for the Coast to call them, had been one of few compensating features; this strange race fascinated her and Stiller, but necessarily from a distance. Now she was working with one in close-up. All her other leading men up to then had been either Swedes or Americans like Moreno and Cortez who posed as fiery Latins. Gilbert had the dash and pep of the real article. His self-charging energy was a potent influence on a woman whose own batteries swiftly ran down. She had only been on nodding terms with Gilbert before director Clarence Brown introduced them on the set of *Flesh and the Devil*. But she had instant praise for the very qualities he had and she had not. 'He has such vitality, spirits, eagerness! Every morning at nine o'clock, he would slip to work opposite me. He was so nice that I felt better; felt a little closer to a strange America.'

Their love scenes in the film were the stuff of which publicists dream: but it is wrong to dismiss them as merely such. It is easy to understand how this unabashed romantic and the intuitive *passionaria* brought each other up to mutual pitch. 'He is so fine an artist', she said, 'that he lifts me up and carries me along with him. It is not just a scene I am doing – I am living.' And living at a romantic pace which would have made the middle-aged Mauritz Stiller pant to match. In their love scenes, she is already granted what would become hers by right, the dominant position: Gilbert's head lies in her lap, her arm encircling it, the physical posture suggesting the man's enslavement to his passions. Garbo's passion has a physical abrasiveness for which her feminine looks leave one unprepared: she rubs her cheek against Gilbert's, as if to create erotic static between them. There are few scenes in American films, silent or talkie, in which two fully-clothed people generate so much sexual desire through simple physical contiguity. They released such a carnal charge that MGM had to devise a happy – i.e. 'moral' – ending. Clarence Brown wanted it to end with the shot of Garbo falling through the ice, thus freeing Gilbert and Hanson to revive the platonic friendship that her destructive love had sundered. MGM tacked on a happier-than-warranted conclusion, showing a frisky Gilbert making up to a new girl.

But the studio was amazed and delighted by one piece of evidence that Garbo's extraordinary acting provided. In the scene where she turns round the communion cup – which she holds like Salome with John the Baptist's head – so as to drink from the place on the rim that her lover's lips have just touched, Garbo was able, magically, to convert a

Garbo and Gilbert pose for a gag photo in front of the movable flat representing the locomotive in *Flesh and the Devil*. Director Clarence Brown poses as the engineer.

OVERLEAF The communion sequence from *Flesh and the Devil*.

1 As the communion cup passes along

2 the row of worshippers,

3 Gilbert drinks from it.

4 Then Garbo, offered the cup,

5 turns it round to drink

6 from the place her lover's lips touched.

7 Thus does a holy rite

8 become a sensual act defying censorship.

holy rite into a sensual act and *at the same time* deflect the censor's possible objections by rendering the 'sin' almost impalpable. A woman who could sin and suffer simultaneously was a god-send in a censor's world where moral misdeed had to be balanced by statutory repentance or inevitable destruction.

The photographer William Daniels played his part in the illusion that Garbo and Gilbert created by lighting the garden scenery of their early encounter so that every leaf gave off a diffused tingle of sympathy. As Gilbert strikes a match to light the cigarette he has transferred from his dry lips (and one senses the tension in his throat) to her yearning ones, its glowing tip pulsates like an index of their emotions. Daniels had actually secreted a minute light bulb in Gilbert's hand. In view of the way some writers speak of Garbo's 'divinity', it is salutary to be reminded how often in her films she collaborated with human agents, and even torch bulbs.

Off-screen, too, the Garbo–Gilbert pairing had assumed the status of a publicized affair. They dined together; picnicked in the Hollywood hills; he called her 'Flicka'

(from the Swedish for 'girl') and named his schooner *The Temptress* after her last role; she called him 'Yacky' and heard herself described as 'the most alluring creature you have ever seen. Capricious as the devil, whimsical, temperamental and fascinating'. How much Garbo was ever really in love with him is another matter. He gave her pleasure and reassurance, introduced her to an America she had not up to then understood, even extended her knowledge of English. But she was fascinated by what he represented as a star rather than a husband. He had a temperamental nature that she could feel safe with; it was basically immature, even childish. The fans desired stars to fall in love off-screen as well as in their films: Garbo was

ABOVE In a break from filming, Garbo shows co-stars Lars Hanson and John Gilbert the difference between the Continental and American ways of wearing a wedding ring. Fans believed she and Gilbert would soon exchange rings in reality.

OPPOSITE Diffused eroticism in *Flesh and the Devil*: but its source was the tiny light bulb that photographer William Daniels concealed in Gilbert's hand.

being taught about celebrity American-style. If Stiller had been the steely mentor in the world of European art films, Gilbert was the person who coached her in stardom in the Hollywood milieu. They were what could be called passionate friends rather than good lovers. Gilbert often and impulsively told the Press he was going to marry her. John Bainbridge's biography quotes a letter from Garbo to a friend in Sweden about *that*. 'I suppose you have read in the papers about me and a certain actor, but I am not, as they say, "going to get married". But they are crazy about news. That is why they have picked on me.'[11]

Gilbert's affection for her had made him agree to her having equal billing with him on *Flesh and the Devil*'s poster credits. But most things in Hollywood, even love and especially self-love, had their cash value; the big difference in their 'equal' status as stars and their far-from-equal salaries was not lost on Garbo. Gilbert had in enviable measure the power and independence Garbo found it so enervating to be without. He had his own business manager, Harry Edington, whose wife, Barbara Kent, acted a minor role in the film. Gilbert could say no to a script he did not like: Garbo had to take what she was given. Another thing they shared was a dislike of Louis B. Mayer. Mayer disapproved of Gilbert's rakish ways and his defiance of some of the family sanctities so dear to Mayer's heart and hearth. In short, Gilbert knew how to handle the phenomenon of stardom whose force-fed, Hollywood-bred nature was so alien to Garbo. At this crucial point in her career, he taught her how to get her own way.

Mauritz Stiller, meanwhile, was working frenziedly to redeem himself. He had signed the Paramount loan-out on 16 June 1926 and, thanks to efficient planning by Erich Pommer, his work on *Hotel Imperial* showed none of the time-consuming tantrums of *The Temptress*. He finished it on schedule on 25 September 1926: whereupon Jesse Lasky sent Louis B. Mayer a cheque for Stiller's services at $1,500 a week – of which Stiller kept only $500 – and the MGM lawyers noted, 'This closes our contract with Lasky and also our contract with Stiller.' On 17 November 1926, Stiller accepted a settlement of $2,166.66 to discharge MGM 'from and of all claims and demands' arising out of his original contract. His spirits restored by the critical and commercial success of *Hotel Imperial*, he pocketed his pride and prepared to pocket something more substantial by engaging to direct another Paramount picture which he was cynical enough to say in advance would be 'rubbish'. But at least he would go home with a full pocket-book.

Garbo was working out her separate destiny too, unimpressed by the salary rise she got on 18 September 1926, as per contract, to a paltry $600 a week. Her resistance stiffened by Gilbert; counselled unofficially by Harry Edington in ways to enhance her value; depressed by the separation from Stiller, the uncongenial climate, the treadmill quality of stardom and her own physical fatigue, she discovered her most powerful weapon. *The weapon of not caring*. To most stars in receipt of Garbo's instantaneous fame and in possession of her vast talent, the ego would have been central. Bruised it might have been by the inevitable servitude of the Hollywood system, but it would have been speedily nursed back to health by ambition, not to say avarice. With Garbo, it was the reverse. Indifference was the by-product of her meteoric career. No star before or since has been so genuinely indifferent about losing the prize. Either she would have it

on her terms, or not at all; and if it was to be not at all, then so what? Hers was to be the triumph of the apathetic will. It is a matter of record – and even nowadays of bafflement – that she gave it all up fifteen years later while only in her mid-thirties and at the height of her powers. But what is almost completely overlooked is her readiness to give it all up within a year of having gained it.

Having made her demand for $5,000 a week, she went home and waited. And waited. It was a war of nerves: as MGM readied *Flesh and the Devil* for release on a public impatient to see the two Great Lovers they had read about in the papers actually in each other's arms, the studio fretted over not having a follow-up picture in production. They offered Garbo a version of *Anna Karenina*; even Tolstoy's pedigree did not make her falter. Mayer appealed to Sven-Hugo Borg to coax reason into her obdurate head. 'One day in his office we talked about you,' Borg told Garbo, 'and this is what he said to me: "Borg, that girl thinks I am a hard, unreasonable man and that I am paying her a salary far below what she is worth. She forgets that it was I who took all the risk. She has acted like a fool and ought to be spanked [and] unless she behaves herself she will regret it." ' This was hardly the way to progress. Borg's role as the go-between was ambiguous. At the same time as he was reporting Mayer's words to Garbo, he was replying to Garbo's New York attorney, Joseph S. Buhler, 'The difficulties between Miss Garbo and the studio are, in my opinion, the fault of Miss Garbo, but as Mr Louis B. Mayer ... holds Miss Garbo in high regard, I am certain that everything will be brought to a satisfactory conclusion.' Buhler, in a letter dated 1 December 1926, repeated this opinion to Garbo, with the advice that she show this letter to Stiller and sack Borg. 'Had I been employed by her instead of by the studio,' the latter recorded, 'she would have done it.'

Now Mauritz Stiller, from the safety of Paramount, sat down on 18 December 1926 and wrote one of the most

OPPOSITE AND BELOW The lighting that William Daniels created for Garbo's early silent films rendered her more erotic than any spoken dialogue.

OVERLEAF Studio portrait, *c.* 1927. A favourite study from the collection of Garbo's nephew, Sven Gustafsson.

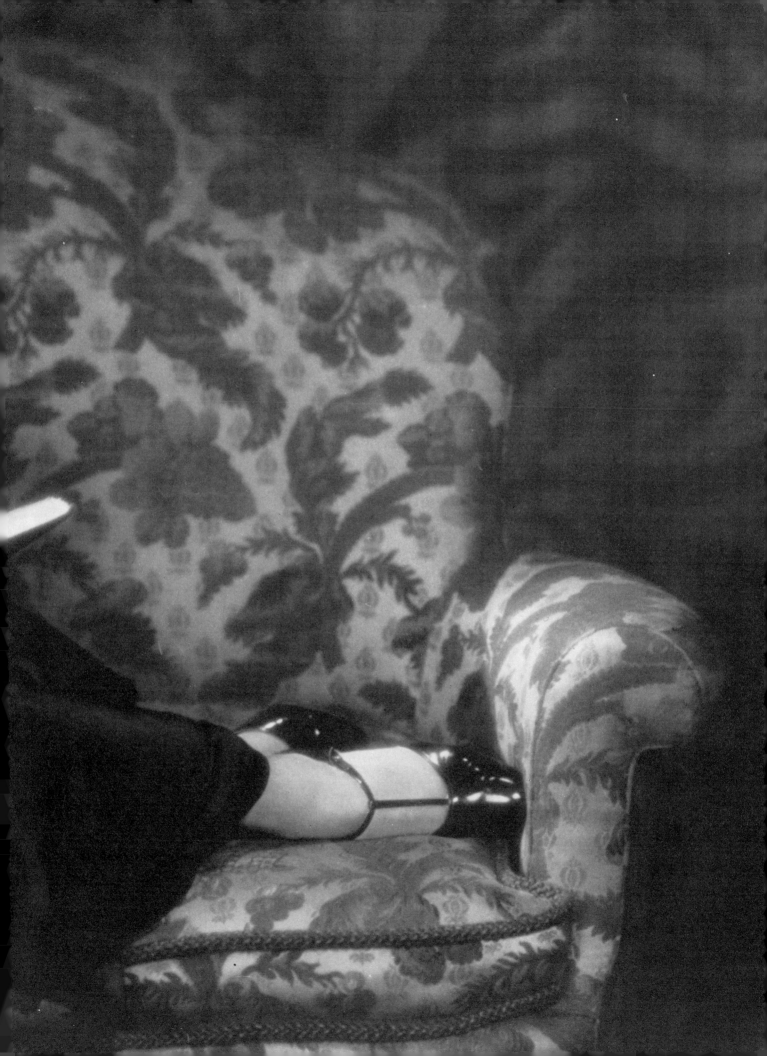

surprising letters that has come to light in the MGM archives.

You doubtless know, Mr Mayer, that Miss Garbo had a much better contract with UFA than the one she now has with your company [Stiller was stretching things: Garbo's contract with UFA was linked to Trianon, and did not survive the production company's bankruptcy] and it was I who persuaded her to accept the lower salary at Metro-Goldwyn-Mayer, because I was directly responsible for her coming to this country, and was absolutely convinced that she would make a wonderful success in America upon her first appearance on the screen. The reason that Miss Garbo has been so unhappy here, notwithstanding her success, is simply the number of vamp roles she has been forced to play and which, she keenly feels, are outside her sphere. You saw her in *Gosta Berling* and you know it was because of her great success in this production that you gave her a contract. In this picture she was an entirely different type – an innocent girl – not a vamp. Believe me or not, Mr Mayer, I have been the only one who consoled her and I explained to her that the first roles she portrayed for your company, whether they were vamp roles or others more suited to her, made absolutely no difference whatsoever. I also told her that I had expressed my opinion to Mr Thalberg and he personally assured me there would be a change and Miss Garbo need have no fear that she had to play vamp roles exclusively in the future . . . . Lately when you wanted to prolong the time of her contract it was I who advised Miss Garbo not to be contrary, but to seriously consider a contract for a longer period of years. At that time I was very busy with my production here and had not a moment to spare, so I advised her to get an attorney. The rest you are well aware of. Personally, I am convinced if Miss Garbo is properly cast she is one of the best attractions a film company can possess and I myself would not hesitate a moment to pay her the amount her representative has asked for, especially when there is an option every year and the firm can terminate her contract practically any time. I have spoken to Miss Garbo and she is willing to sign a five-year contract on the following terms: the first two years $500 less per week, and the remaining three years $1000 less per week than her attorney has requested. This is all I have to say in this case and quite all I have been able to accomplish. I would indeed be very happy if Miss Garbo remained with the firm who first gave her the opportunity to appear before the American public. I sincerely hope when she takes the part of Anna Karenina that this will be the beginning of a bigger era for Metro-Goldwyn-Mayer and Miss Garbo, and that from now on you need not fear further misunderstandings *vis à vis* roles. Sincerely Yours, Mauritz Stiller.

Garbo did not budge from her demand for an immediate raise to $5,000 a week. 'This is the third Christmas away from Sweden,' she wrote home, 'and I feel so unhappy, and treated in such a stepmotherly away. Can you understand it? It is so childish to be that way when one can't go home anyway and ought to be grateful for a position that millions would thank God for. Well, that's how it is.'[12] On 26 February 1927, Mayer suspended her officially, on no pay. On 2 March, Garbo sent a note saying she had not been told

to report for work; but this brought the stiff rebuke from Mayer that such an excuse was 'not in good faith'. She knew she had been cast as Anna Karenina – but she had not tried to communicate till four days later. Perhaps urged on by Gilbert, her strategy mapped out by Edington, Garbo replied at length and with passion in a six-page cable sent on 6 March to J. Robert Rubin, head of all MGM legal affairs, at his New York headquarters. She set forth her fears, claiming that Mayer had threatened her with 'bad parts' for the rest of her three-year contract if she did not sign the new five-year contract he had offered – one 'like the other Metro stars'. 'But', Garbo added, 'I leave it to you to judge if you have ever seen a star contract like that. When the new contract was drawn up, I was playing three roles a year. Because my constitution is not strong and if I were to play as many roles as they see fit I know I would break down under the strain.' She charged that Mayer had made her a verbal promise of more considerate treatment: but it had not been put in the contract. Until all was to her liking, she was not signing.

What broke this impasse was very likely the box-office returns of *Flesh and the Devil*, which had opened on 9 January 1927. They were sensational enough to make the studio consider it better to yield to Garbo and make another fortune than resist her demands and lose one. Hence a new twelve-page contract was signed on 1 June 1927 – a remarkable one for a player who had made only three films, been in Hollywood less than two years, and held the most powerful company there to virtual ransom. Back-dated to 1 January 1927, it hoisted Garbo's salary from $600 to $2,000 a week. It provided for a two-week lay-off: but Charles A. Green noted, 'she is to be continued on salary until we have Mayer's instructions regarding lay-off' (a pencilled note adds: 'Approved, Louis B. Mayer'). There were further enriching options: a second year at $4,000 a week; a third at $5,000 a week; a fourth at $6,000 a week. No lay-offs at any time. Only the 'million-dollar contract' that Edington had negotiated for John Gilbert exceeded these terms. He took no fee for handling Garbo's affairs, though there exists evidence that the studio made it up to him in other ways and at least one memo refers to the $20,000 paid to Edington for every picture Garbo made. But the gain to him in prestige was immense, and at once played its part in the evolving Garbo image.

To underline her exclusiveness, and so authenticate his own prestige, Edington immediately curtailed all publicity of a sort he deemed cheapening. No more interviews, unless he sanctioned them and she agreed. As this coincided exactly with her own distaste for publicity (as well as her poor technique in handling it), she readily assented. Stiller and Edington were not the only people who advised her to make herself unavailable to Press and public. Lon Chaney, the 'Man of a Thousand Faces', knew the commercial value of keeping the public guessing which face was really his in his MGM melodramas. To a woman with one face like Garbo, he advised keeping the public guessing about what lay behind it. Sven-Hugo Borg also claimed that he insinuated into her receptive mind the idea that she make professional use of her personal inclination for seclusion. 'As we lay on the beach at Santa Monica one day, I said to her: "I know you are not acting, Greta, when you hide from people; but just the same, it is something that fits your personality, to be mysterious and secretive. By playing up to it . . . you will get your privacy and also get

people talking about you." "You think so, Borg," she said slowly. "Yes, maybe it is a good idea." ' Now she had Harry Edington acting as her intermediary with the world; his wife, the actress Barbara Kent, gradually became Garbo's unofficial secretary, dealing with all her correspondence, and isolating her in fact as well as appearance from the intrusive world. Seeking to raise her into what would now be called superstardom, Edington ordained another change in her status. Henceforth, where possible, she would be billed simply as 'Garbo'. Like 'Duse' or 'Bernhardt', the goddess should have no commonplace appurtenance like a Christian name: what need was there to identify her further? She was unique.

Anna Karenina was premièred on 29 November 1927, its title having been changed to *Love* so that it could be billed as 'John Gilbert and Greta Garbo in *Love*'. (Mayer had personally favoured a title-change to *Sacred and Profane Love*: his advisers wooed him away from this by stressing the succinctness of the undifferentiated passion in display advertising.) During filming Gilbert tried eloping with Garbo: but the grand passion off-screen turned into the sort of screwball comedy that the next decade enjoyed *on* it. Garbo took fright as they neared the Long Beach home of a Justice of the Peace, bolted into a ladies' room and boarded the train home.

More revealing than the love scenes between the adults in the film are the extraordinarily 'sexy' scenes between Garbo's Anna and the ten-year-old Philippe de Lacy who plays her son. ('At twenty-two, I have a son of ten – funny,

OPPOSITE Advice from the 'Man of a Thousand Faces'. Lon Chaney, in costume for *The Road to Mandalay*, visits Stiller, Garbo, Niblo and Moreno on the set of *The Temptress*.

ABOVE With Philippe de Lacy in *Love*: a passion-starved mother turns her son into a substitute love-object.

OVERLEAF Encounter in the woods in *Love*.

huh?' Garbo commented.) Dietrich and Garbo had this in common: outwardly *femmes fatales* in their films, women of the world who sought out the little boy in the men who pursued them, they could deploy their femininity in scenes with children in such a way as to summon forth and flatter the latent manhood of their screen offspring. The flirtatious de Lacy, a remarkable child actor who resembles a male Shirley Temple, behaves like a miniature adult: and the love-starved Anna turns him into a substitute love-object. Garbo always felt safest with children, on screen and off. 'They don't get too close to you,' she said – i.e., they don't threaten your private feelings. 'They act rationally and with commonsense' – i.e., unlike most of the wearisome adults she dealt with. 'When you talk silly things, they just look at you, and you feel they are thinking, "What are you saying such silly things for?" ' – i.e., like Garbo, children kept their thoughts to themselves. In almost every man

with whom Garbo associated publicly in later years, there was an element of the child.

In the aftermath of the 'exclusiveness' now cast around her like a security blanket, MGM's choice for her next film suggests how art was starting to borrow from life, or, at least, from the idea that Garbo's public had of her life. *The Divine Woman* (14 January 1928) is, tragically, the one film of hers that has been lost. All prints and even the negative have disappeared, to date, anyhow. This is doubly unfortunate. Contemporary critics remarked how Garbo's range of effects had widened in it. The reviewer of *Motion*

OPPOSITE *Love*, 1927. John Gilbert, as Vronsky, sees the reflection of destiny.

BELOW Destiny in the flesh: Garbo as Anna Karenina in the silent version of Tolstoy's novel.

Picture wrote: 'Given a part in which she is expected to be something more than a vamp, she is quite a capable girl.' The remark reminds us that even as early as 1927 there was a small but tenacious anti-Garbo lobby reluctant to admit that Garbo could *act*, that she was more than a beautiful woman with a strong appeal. Secondly, the film gave Garbo's countryman Victor Seastrom his one and only opportunity to direct her.

The screenplay for *The Divine Woman* (dated 12 September 1927) and the cutting continuity script (11 January 1928), which departs from it only in tone and emphasis, follow the story of a French peasant girl momentarily transformed into her country's greatest

LEFT A lunchbreak during location shooting on *Love* for photographer William Daniels, director Edmund Goulding, Garbo, Gilbert and two unidentified guests.

BELOW Garbo as the innocent French peasant girl Marah, 'her eyes full of wonder' as she tries on her courtesan mother's jewels in *The Divine Woman*. It is the only film she made with her countryman Victor Seastrom, and the only film of hers which has been lost.

OVERLEAF With co-star Lars Hanson. Despite the title, critics praised the unanticipated humanity of Garbo's acting: she was no longer the other-worldly vamp. But the love scenes with Hanson, besides being provocatively 'horizontal', confirmed Garbo's dominance in matters of passion.

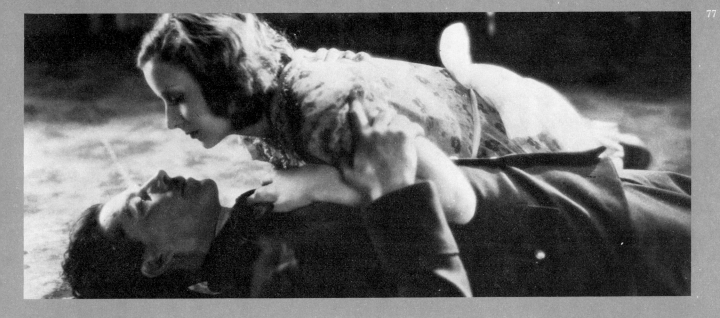

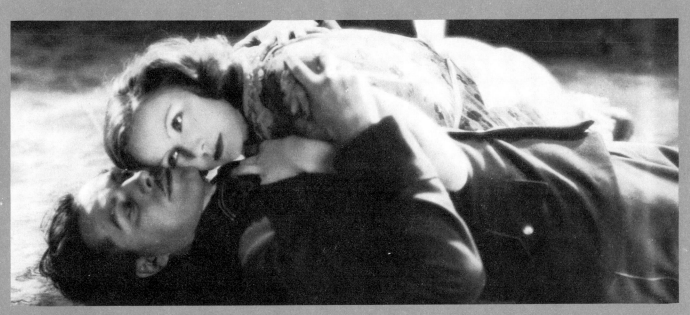

actress, but giving it all up for the love of an Army deserter who murmurs, 'There's a ranch in South America – and a garden waiting for you.' The first thing to state, beyond the triteness that Garbo and Lars Hanson undoubtedly transformed with Seastrom's help, is that the title's intentional echo of the Sarah Bernhardt attribute is totally misleading. There is no other connection between the film's Marah (re-named Marianne in the finished print) and the Divine Sarah. But Dorothy Farnum's screenplay appears to enlist just those things that Garbo was now well known for doing uniquely well. One 'sees' her vivid physical presence in the script's description of the peasant girl's first appearance in her courtesan mother's Paris home: 'A strange creature has invaded Rosine's drawing-room – a young girl in the quaint but clumsy costume of the Province of Auvergne. She is moving like a humming bird from one lovely thing to another. She smooths a silken curtain, she reaches on tiptoes to touch the glittering crystals of the chandelier. THE CAMERA MOVES UP CLOSER. She walks to a magnificent mirror. THE CAMERA KEEPS MOVING UP until it holds her in CLOSE UP just as she looks at herself in the mirror. For the first time we have seen her face. She is Marah, and her eyes are full of wonder.'

Mauritz Stiller had tried to return to MGM to direct *The Divine Woman* – it might have made the perfect 'peace-making' material – but his health was by now not up to it. His career had drooped again. He had badly missed Erich Pommer's orderly and steadying hand in his second Paramount picture, *Barbed Wire*; he went to pieces a few days after starting to shoot *The Street of Sin* and was replaced by Lothar Mendes with part-time help from Josef von Sternberg – the man who later made the crude, inaccurate claim in his memoirs that it was he who advised Louis B. Mayer 'to import Mauritz Stiller and ask him to include Greta Garbo in his luggage'.[13] Dispirited and sickening, Stiller sailed for Sweden in November 1927.

Garbo's temperament was changing, slowly but noticeably. More than ever, it was dictating her daily moods and decisions. In spite of getting her own way, she enjoyed no sense of triumph. MGM executive memos now begin to refer to her in terms of extreme gingerliness. She was still obstinate: now she had become unpredictable. Mercedes de Acosta saw Garbo's moodiness at a well-developed stage and wrote, 'She could be gay and look well and within five minutes she would be desperately depressed and apparently terribly ill.'[14] She had been dieting with what the studio feared was dangerous disregard for her health. Once she had been suspended; now she had to be rested.

Between completing photography of *The Divine Woman*, on 7 November 1927, and beginning her next role in *The Mysterious Lady*, on 8 May 1928, there occurred an

OPPOSITE *The Divine Woman* had Garbo revert to a more statuesque pose when the character became the toast of Europe.

BELOW One famous face contemplates another: in *The Mysterious Lady*, Garbo was so brilliantly photographed that her exhaustion passed for sexual longing.

OVERLEAF Shooting *The Mysterious Lady*. Garbo, on the staircase, is with Conrad Nagel. The musicians are not part of the scene, but the silent film era's method of inducing the mood in the actors by playing appropriate melodies.

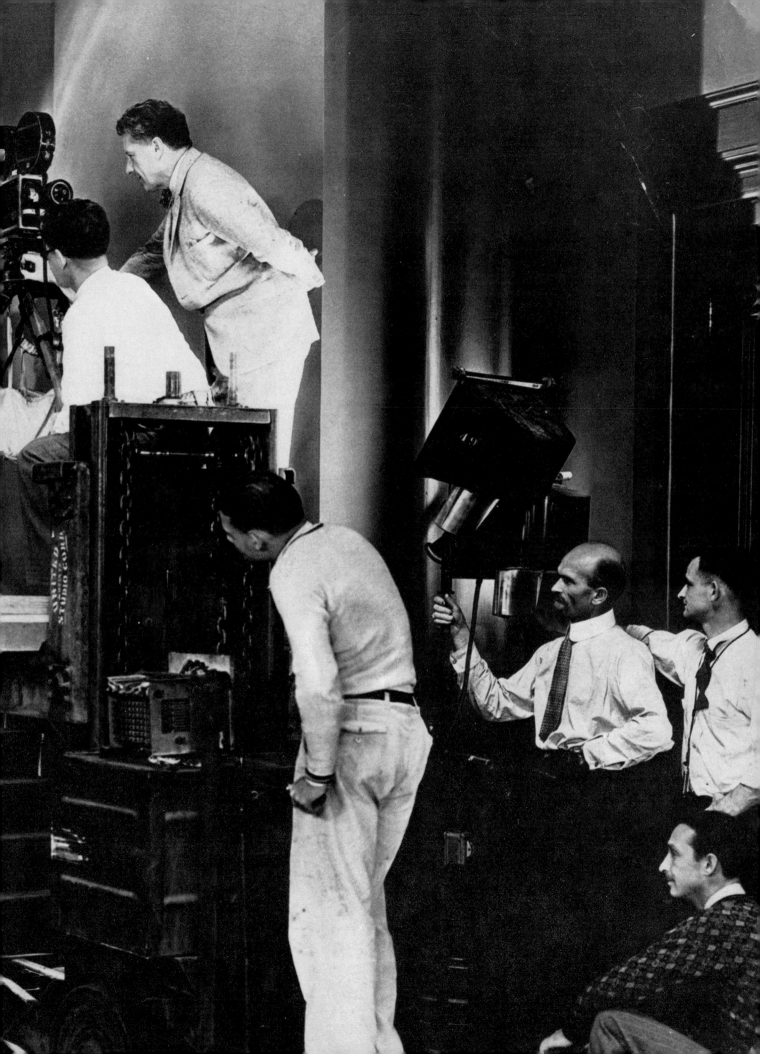

OPPOSITE, TOP 'There are love scenes by the score,' said a critic. With Conrad Nagel.

OPPOSITE, BOTTOM LEFT A spy story, *The Mysterious Lady* took every chance to reflect Garbo's duplicity in ornate looking-glasses.

LEFT Her very pose as she opens the door of spymaster Gustav von Seyffertitz's study is provocative, never mind the suggestive dress.

ABOVE, LEFT AND RIGHT Garbo could turn loneliness into a form of tragic depression.

unusually long interval for an artist on full pay with no lay-off sanctions. Never again did she look as tired on the screen as she did in Fred Niblo's picture about a secret agent who shoots her spymaster in order to save her enemy lover. As she lets herself into her apartment, she leans leadenly against the wall; after she has shown her lover out, she again presses herself against the door as if it were his body. No film so clearly shows that, for Garbo, passion was a form of tragic depression. The tiredness in her face is converted, with William Daniels' lighting, into romantic agony. The way other people turned calories into energy, Garbo turned the lack of them into love-sickness.

She had recovered her energies by the time she played Iris March, the doomed flapper-girl heroine of Michael Arlen's *succès de scandale*, *The Green Hat*, for which MGM paid a breathtaking $50,250, then re-naming it *A Woman of Affairs* and at the same time cleansing its plot of the element of syphilis and substituting embezzlement and suicide. It is her first role that is really contemporary in feel. Instead of the grand romantic line, Garbo plays the part in modern shorthand. Applying lipstick, expelling cigarette smoke in a quick stream, whipping off her cloche hat as she gets behind the wheel of her Hispano-Suiza so as to feel the wind and be in direct contact with life, she treats each action as if it has to be finished quickly – as if life itself might leave no time for its completion.

But the film would be worth treasuring even if it contained nothing else except the hallucinatory scene in hospital, when Garbo is visited by John Gilbert while recovering from a nervous collapse. After he has been to her bedside, Gilbert reports back to his wife that she does not know him. Suddenly Garbo appears at the doorway, and advances towards the bouquet he has brought, seeing only the flowers, everything else being unfocused. Sweeping up the flowers, she presses them to her body like a woman with her lover, plunges her face deeply into them, inhaling strength from them, and finally bears the bouquet back to her room pressed close to her cheek like a new-born baby in that hospital setting. It is one of the greatest transformation effects in Garbo's repertoire: second only to the famous furniture-touching sequence in *Queen Christina*. Charles Affron, in his study *Star Acting*, calls attention to the subtle way Garbo used her left hand like an

OPPOSITE Garbo's entrances were always carefully designed. The neurotic drive of her performance as Michael Arlen's liberated woman in the 1920s in *A Woman of Affairs* redeems a film that censorship had bowdlerized.

BELOW AND RIGHT The ever-loyal William Daniels photographs Garbo and Gilbert in the fateful Hispano-Suiza.

OVERLEAF A sequence from *A Woman of Affairs*.

1 Garbo, sick in hospital: 'Where are my flowers?'

2

3 Seeing only Gilbert's bouquet,

4 she embraces them as if they were her lover,

5 transmitting her own emotions to the object,

6 sustained by the faithful Lewis Stone.

7 Then, seeing Gilbert, she transfers her affections.

8 Garbo: 'I don't want much – only you.'

R.²⁶/₁₀ 28.G

orchestra baton 'constantly modulating the reaction' and giving herself the internal rhythm of the scene.[15] In *Queen Christina*, a real metronome was used: but the effect is hardly more marvellous.

On New Year's Eve, 1927, a journalist called Ruth Biery sat at a table in a tiny tea-room in Santa Monica talking to Greta Garbo, who had just thrown from her shoulders a grey woolly coat ' " such as we wear in Sweden", and was looking wistfully out of the window as though to penetrate the dark secrets beyond them. "Let's not talk of me!" she pleaded.' She pleaded, it need hardly be said, in vain. This was the longest and the last face-to-face interview that Greta Garbo was to give for many, many years. It was a prestigious piece because of its rarity value even then, and was run over three issues – April, May and June 1928 – in the leading film magazine *Photoplay*. Like all Garbo interviews, it has a sub-text that emerges revealingly in the context of the studio power-play and the image-building campaign that Harry Edington was now masterminding. Edington had set the interview up, as one can infer from a fulsome tribute to him that must have aroused cynical laughter among the studio heads: 'Mr Edington makes us all understand one another [at MGM] and we are all very happy.' Garbo's growing perverseness is the next thing that emerges in her refusal to cite even the commonest family details. 'My brother's name? My sister's? . . . . What does that matter? They are *my* people. Why should I tell their names to other people? Names do not matter. If I should read them – it would hurt.' Already cross-grained by temperament, Garbo was becoming more so by intention, beginning to make secrets where none need exist. By refusing to disclose even the commonest bits of information, she was finding a fascinatingly negative way of asserting herself. It was a remote attitude, in sharp contrast to the homely note most Hollywood stars then attempted to strike with the Press. Another kind of remoteness soon appeared. Asked about rumours of marriage, she replied: 'Love? Of course I have been in love. Who hasn't been in love? Marriage? I have told many times, I do not know. I like to be alone: not always with the same person.' Good friends were to be preferred to constant husbands: she spoke warmly of Emil Jannings, the recent German 'import' to Hollywood, and said admiringly of Mrs Jannings, '[she] is a real woman', meaning, she explained, 'she means what she says'. The qualities Garbo admired in her very few close friends obviously reflected her own stiffening temperament.

The article was illustrated by a number of artist's sketches: Garbo all alone at her drama school audition; Garbo in Constantinople for the aborted *Odalisque* movie, aimlessly following a Turkish mendicant, who, like her, 'did not have anywhere to go but wander'; Garbo on the Santa Monica beach. They all emphasized her loneliness and, by extension, her mystery. *Why* is this beautiful, desirable, famous woman alone? At the end of the interview, she provided that 'glimpse of infinity' feeling her scriptwriters strove to provide at the tragic or happy endings to her movies. 'I never know what I am going to do next when I am not working.' What had begun as an indifference to consequences would, in the years ahead, change perceptibly into an indecisiveness about actions.

It was in the middle of her next film, *Wild Orchids* (30 March 1929), that a cable arrived from Victor Seastrom, who was in Stockholm, informing her that Mauritz Stiller had died. It was 8 November 1928: he was forty-five. He left no will and his principal creditor, Svensk Filmindustri, claimed most of the cash on deposit in Sweden and America. When Garbo got the news, in the middle of a love scene with her co-star Nils Asther, she turned deathly pale, walked off the set, steadied herself against the flats, then returned to finish the scene. Asther has recalled that he later heard helpless laughter coming from her dressing-room. When he entered at her call, Garbo was in near-hysterics over a small bottle no bigger than a perfume flacon, containing brandy and carrying the accompanying card: 'Dear Greta. My sympathy in your sorrow. But the show must go on. Louis B. Mayer.' Mayer had balanced precisely the obligation to show sympathy with the prudent amount of liquor that Prohibition might pardonably permit in such grief. That all was far from healed between Garbo and Mayer emerged in a cable despatched by him personally a few weeks later, on 3 December 1928, addressed to 'Drawing-room A, Car 206, Train 20 "The Chief" ', rebuking her for leaving the production before the retakes had been made. Those schedules for that day, he told her, could be done in time for her to make the connection at New York with the Sweden-bound liner.

'There is still time for you to return to Culver City . . . and make Sweden in time for Christmas. Return or great loss and damage will be caused us.' She did not return. Accordingly, he suspended her without pay on 5 December, three days before she sailed home for her first visit to her native country in three-and-a-half years.

While in Stockholm, where she found her celebrity was as bothersome as in Hollywood, and could be protected far less successfully from prying cameramen, she made a sombre excursion. Mauritz Stiller's lawyer has recalled how he accompanied her to the store-room where his late client's effects were being kept. 'I remember vividly how she walked about the room, touching this item and that. "This was the suitcase he bought in America," she said,

OPPOSITE, TOP Garbo (left) with two of her closest friends, German actor Emil Jannings and his wife, *c.* 1928. Talkies were soon to send Jannings back to Europe.

OPPOSITE, BOTTOM Just before Christmas 1928, Garbo, now a world-famous star, returns to Europe herself. Mimi Pollak (behind) greets her old classmate on the Stockholm-bound boat-train.

BELOW The star and her mother ride home in triumph. For once, Garbo bore fame with a smile.

picking up the bag. "And those rugs – I remember when he bought them in Turkey." We stayed quite a time while she walked round the furniture and paintings and made sad little moments.'[16] Five years later she did her celebrated furniture-touching sequence in *Queen Christina*. Did the sensory immediacy of that bedchamber scene, in which the inventory of love objects takes on the pathetic character of *memento mori*, owe anything to her last sad contact with the man who had been her discoverer, friend, mentor and maybe lover? One would like to think so. She also visited his grave in the Jewish cemetery; and perhaps it is appropriate to point out how many people who knew Garbo well, as a friend or fellow worker, all agree on her tenacious pro-Jewish sympathies. That story of her wanting to seek an interview with Hitler and shoot him with a concealed pistol may not be a piece of Mata Hari-like apocrypha after all.

Wild Orchids had been her first American film to cast her as an undeniably 'good woman', standing by her marriage contract to ageing Lewis Stone instead of surrendering

OPPOSITE With Nils Asther, as a Javanese prince, in *Wild Orchids*.

ABOVE In the middle of making *Wild Orchids*, Garbo got the news of Mauritz Stiller's death. She warned her co-stars Lewis Stone and Nils Asther: 'You will have something dead on the screen. It will have no life.' She was not entirely wrong.

LEFT Cast in *Wild Orchids* as an undeniably 'good' woman, Garbo now suffers other lovers' unsought torments.

(willingly at least) to Nils Asther's rather puppyish Oriental potentate. It proved that happiness was not her forte. Nor was it what her public expected. When Garbo appears at the beginning as a merrily laughing young wife, some filmgoers believed a double had been used. Passion, not mirth, was the public's demand. As a film, it is memorable chiefly for Daniels' lush lighting effects and the many moods in which he drenches Garbo, including the dramatic moment when Nils Asther's bedroom door opens, flooding Garbo with light, and, in Richard Corliss's words, 'his shadow crawls up her body'.

On her return to New York, on 19 March 1929, she said she would like to play Joan of Arc, or 'something unusual, something that has not been done before'. Instead, she was put straight into *The Single Standard* (27 July 1929) as Arden Stuart, San Francisco débutante and 'New Woman'. Interesting now are the ways in which Garbo's moody life is increasingly conscripted by the screenwriters to pander to audiences' knowingness (or what they believed to be such) about Garbo. She spends much of the film walking in the rain (a favourite pastime), her umbrella a surprisingly utilitarian object to find in her romantic grip. She tells a person who accosts her, 'I am walking alone because I want to be alone.' Dozens of reporters had already encountered that blunt put-down. She meets an artist, an ex-boxer played by Nils Asther, with the amorous good looks of John Gilbert and a yacht called *The All Alone*. But marital fidelity and maternal love – Arden has got married to the usual nondescript bore who was Garbo's

implausible preference as a husband-type in film after film – cause him to sail away past her window while she cries through her laughter. Censorship was now prescribing the ending of Garbo's films, modulating their previous sinful fatefulness into a bourgeois compliance with the Hays Office code. Maybe *The Single Standard* would have had more fire, had it co-starred John Gilbert and thus re-heated the romantic embers. But Gilbert got married (to Ina Claire) while Garbo was making it. To the reporter who appeared on location at Catalina Island bearing the headlined news, she answered neutrally: 'Thank you. I hope Mr Gilbert will be very happy.' A year or two later, Gilbert said, in what one must infer to be wishful thinking, 'I think she has always been lonely for me.' If so, she gave no indication of the direction of her longings; the American male was no longer the child-like novelty he had been for her. Garbo was settling in.

Harry Edington, concerned for her prestige, had persuaded her to move from Santa Monica's beach hotel to the Beverly Hills Hotel; but before long an over-zealous

ABOVE Garbo's appearance as a light-hearted newly-wed at the start of *Wild Orchids* disconcerted her public. They expected her usual brand of resigned fatalism.

OPPOSITE After Stiller's death, Garbo withdrew more and more from the world. Here she rests between takes for *The Single Standard*, on Catalina Island.

OVERLEAF As Arden Stuart, San Francisco débutante and 'New Woman' in *The Single Standard*.

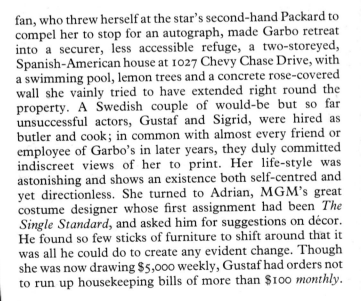

fan, who threw herself at the star's second-hand Packard to compel her to stop for an autograph, made Garbo retreat into a securer, less accessible refuge, a two-storeyed, Spanish-American house at 1027 Chevy Chase Drive, with a swimming pool, lemon trees and a concrete rose-covered wall she vainly tried to have extended right round the property. A Swedish couple of would-be but so far unsuccessful actors, Gustaf and Sigrid, were hired as butler and cook; in common with almost every friend or employee of Garbo's in later years, they duly committed indiscreet views of her to print. Her life-style was astonishing and shows an existence both self-centred and yet directionless. She turned to Adrian, MGM's great costume designer whose first assignment had been *The Single Standard*, and asked him for suggestions on décor. He found so few sticks of furniture to shift around that it was all he could do to create any evident change. Though she was now drawing $5,000 weekly, Gustaf had orders not to run up housekeeping bills of more than $100 *monthly*.

ABOVE Nils Asther, looking remarkably like her old love John Gilbert, co-starred with Garbo again in *The Single Standard*.

LEFT While filming this sequence aboard Asther's yacht, Garbo got the news of Gilbert's remarriage. She calmly sent her wishes for his happiness.

OPPOSITE Perhaps reflecting sterner censorship taboos, the film charted Garbo's progress from a fun-loving girl who impulsively seduces her chauffeur (top) to becoming a wiser and less worldly figure (left) who finds marriage and child (right) more important than romantic flings.

430-3

Fortunately, there was little reciprocal entertaining! He pinned each receipt to the appropriate page in a little black book which Garbo furnished for his use and her scrutiny. Like many people not accustomed to sizeable sums of money, she dealt more expeditiously with smaller amounts. Gustaf Norin recalled he sometimes got refunds on magazines he had bought which were found on inspection to contain nothing about his famous employer. Despite her genuine fear of the way journalists might take advantage of her vulnerability, Garbo read (and still reads avidly) what they wrote about her. Her mother mailed her bundles of European magazines (all her mail, except letters with secret markings, were re-routed to Edington's office, just as in later years the Swedish Consulate in New York would 'accept' mail sent to her in that city), and the MGM office in Paris sent her the new French, German or Swedish novels, particularly any on which the studio had an option.

Garbo never answered the telephone: Gustaf had instructions to say 'Mr Norin's residence' until the caller proved to be *persona grata*. She was usually awakened at 7.00 a.m. – or, to be accurate, she ate her breakfast then, for her insomnia had become permanent, despite her efforts to

ABOVE AND LEFT The art deco designs of *The Single Standard* proved Garbo's innate capacity to adapt her looks to any period and strike postures that were intimate, yet matter of fact, and as much in the modern Twenties manner as her more theatrical vamp roles. With John Mack Brown.

OPPOSITE A very rare picture of Garbo with MGM's great costume designer Gilbert Adrian. She fired his imagination; and when Garbo quit films, Adrian quit MGM too, claiming that the glamour was over.

encourage sleep with warm baths, late snacks and soporific drinks. Paradoxically, her morning appetite was hearty; worry and tension burned away her calories, for weight was never a problem, as she tucked into a breakfast that was on heavy Scandinavian lines rather than those of Continental frugality: fruit juice, a grapefruit, creamed chipped beef, fried potatoes, an egg, coffee and coffee cake, eaten off chinaware given her by Emil Jannings. Gustaf has recalled that she took 80 per cent of her meals in bed: 'she needed a lot of rest'. She smoked heavily, liked playing the phonograph and was fond of Sophie Tucker, and read her servant's own copy of the *Times-Examiner*. Exercise was something she took when other Californians were not around, which was the practical reason for stalking through the rain in a slicker and seaworthy hat, or hiking through the semi-rural acres of Beverly Hills by moonlight: Californians preferred dry days and sunlight. She liked horseback riding; but invariably she settled the monthly account in ready cash, so as not to have to reveal her address to the stable owner. Characteristically, she negotiated a special rate. She also bounced a 15-lb medicine ball around (none too accurately, Gustaf reflected, remembering crushed flower beds). She had several pets: a chow called Flimsy given her by Emil Jannings' daughter, two cats

ABOVE AND LEFT Despite her basic dislike of clothes, Garbo could wear any Adrian costume as though born to it, like this casually elegant creation for *The Single Standard*.

OPPOSITE Garbo in the practical kind of outfit she wore in private life. She is seen here in 1932 on one of her return trips to Sweden.

named Big Pint and Half Pint, and a parrot called, conventionally, Polly, whom she tried to coax into a return-from-work croak of 'Hello, Greta.'

Garbo's wardrobe was spartan and piecemeal. For practical reasons, she preferred men's pyjamas; the men's shirts and ties she wore fitted both her flat chest and her concept of quick dressing, uncomplicated living and unprovocative fashion-sense. In cold weather she wore light-weight woollen stockings; in hot, lisle half-socks. Gustaf brought several pairs of men's oxfords (smallest size) back from the sales. According to him, she would say, 'Just the thing for us bachelors, eh, Gustaf?' She suffered from sinus troubles, caught cold easily and used herbal infusions for relief and, more surprisingly, went to a Turkish bath near the studio where, in the anonymity of a large bath towel, she was seldom recognized. Sometimes she would rub her face with ice-chips in the morning (in *Queen Christina*, a handful of snow is pressed into service for a brief, orgasmic-like rub). No cold cream or any other cosmetics except lavender soap. If she used perfume, it was gardenia. Her hair rinse was camomile tea imported from England – the extent of her luxury.

Yet Garbo was no hermit. 'For a Swede it is just as natural to be alone as it is for an American to "get together",' she said on one occasion. Her closest friends were expatriates like herself: Jacques Feyder, Françoise Rosay, the Emil Jannings, the British actor John Loder and his Austrian wife. 'In the year and a half I have known her,' Loder confided to a journalist, 'I cannot remember that she ever made one definite appointment, even a dinner engagement, a day in advance.' She preferred to appear on people's doorsteps unannounced, invariably uninvited.

Virgilia Peterson Ross opened a short profile of the star in *The New Yorker* by describing her unexpected arrival at a Hollywood party: 'She sat silent while they made sporadic comments on the weather and stole furtive looks at her. She was alone, bottled in by a childish lack of interest, inarticulate, uncomfortable, offering no access to herself. She was unwilling, perhaps unable to share in the social responsibilities of the occasion. She had made every effort to come and now, awkwardly, she hid behind her beauty. The party soon scattered. Garbo had frozen the evening.'[17] When such comments began to appear in print, Garbo's feeling that the Press were too intrusive was overtaken by the impression that they were actually bent on persecuting her. She preferred to draw round her the protective cordon of intimates – if they could be unnoticed. This generally meant choosing 'show business restaurants' on her nights out: Musso-Frank's, the Apex (a coloured club whose blues music she liked), the Russian Eagle (a night-club specializing in Slav dishes). She went to Long Beach or Santa Monica cinemas, usually to mid-week matinées where the chance of being recognized was reduced. (Her favourite actor was Gary Cooper; she admired Ernst Lubitsch and after seeing *The Love Parade* paid a surprise call on him at home. 'Greta,' he said, 'why don't you tell those idiots at your studio to let us do a picture together?' Garbo answered, 'Ernst, you tell them. I am far too tired to have a conversation with any studio executive.')

The theatre presented tougher problems of concealment – and of dress. When she decided to attend the first performance by the dancer Argentina, she wore the top of a gold lamé pair of lounging pyjamas and a short black skirt that no one could have mistaken for an evening gown – she

relied on the theatre box to cover its brevity. John Loder reported: 'She reserved seats at the rear of a box. We crept in unnoticed. Soon it seemed as if all the opera glasses in the audience were turned on our box instead of the stage. There was a noticeable murmur of whispers. When Greta commenced to fidget with her hands, I knew she was annoyed. During intermission we stepped out into the narrow hall back of the box. Two lines formed to pass her. Ten minutes before the final curtain, we quietly slipped out. I heard, later, that at the close of the performance crowds lined the street in front of the theatre, as word had gone round that Garbo was in the audience.'[18]

One of the few recorded snubs she received came from Françoise Rosay. Her friend William Sorensen, a young Swede she had met on her first visit home who followed her back to Hollywood, had accepted a dinner invitation from Rosay and her husband Jacques Feyder. 'Garbo seemed to congeal at the news that I was going out to dinner without her. "Why can't the two of us go out together?" "Because I've accepted. I can't go on cancelling engagements because of you." She drummed her fingers for a moment and then said, "Call them and say I'll be coming with you." "No," I replied, "call them yourself. They're already offended at you for not coming last time." Garbo made the telephone call . . . and was told she could come, but the tone of Françoise Rosay's voice had an edge to it.' The rebuke stung Garbo to the quick and she dressed to kill for once in her life – black tailored dress, mascara, powder. She was impatient on the way to the house and, on entering, cried out 'Ich bin ganz und gar besoffen' ('I am stinking drunk'). Rosay replied, 'Greta, never mind. Sie herzliches willkommen to you just the same.'

Her sense of humour was usually of the inadvertent kind which seemed funny to people because the words came from Greta Garbo and played against her reputation for mystery and remoteness. But she could be penetrating on occasion. Once, when she was looking for a new home – a search that developed into a mania for moving throughout the 1930s as each house she inhabited for a year or so, became too well-known or, she suspected, too exposed to prying eyes – she was shown round a floridly decorated house just vacated by Charlie Chaplin and his child-wife, Lita Grey Chaplin. In the library was an automated organ. Garbo laughed. 'Everything's mechanical – just like he is.' She liked going on long, aimless shopping expeditions, usually buying small, cheap inessentials – after all, what was essential? Shopping was a means of putting in time, of purchasing jokey, trumpery items that would do as tokens of the affection she was too shy to express in words.

Shyness determined her social life as tiredness did her working day. There are few accounts of her ever entertaining anyone, and her friends were surprised to be invited to her home for Christmas Day, 1930. With curtains drawn against the sunshine, candles burning, holly twigs inserting a touch of Northern climate amongst the Californian poinsettias, the guests ate a meal that started with a twenty-two-dish smorgasbord, went on to roast goose (her favourite dish) and ended with apple cake and aquavit, and a swim in the pool. 'Greta got a great kick out of going for a swim on Christmas Day,' Loder recalled. Whether at home, work or on vacation, she stubbornly refused to meet

RIGHT *The Kiss*, premièred in 1929, was Garbo's last silent film.

anyone she saw no reason to meet: Lady Mountbatten ('She would stare at me working'), Mary Pickford ('Why is she interested in me?'), Douglas Fairbanks Sr. ('He makes me feel tired'). She especially shunned celebrities who wrote for magazines: to them she would be not just an object of curiosity, but a source of profit.

Garbo's last silent film, *The Kiss* (15 November 1929), cast her opposite an unusually youthful leading man, Lew Ayres. It is interesting to observe how she coped with this, seeming to alter the specific gravity of her body, never mind her personality, by making it light, buoyant and radiant one minute so as to match Ayres' puppy-like charm, then restoring its gravity as the heavier weight of romance with Conrad Nagel confronts her. Early in the film, she kills her husband as he is about to attack Ayres. It is a shock, supplemented by William Daniels' overhead camera shot, to see Garbo on her knees, in a panic, lunging forward with the momentum of her grossly-built husband's body to restrain his assault. It is the only scene in her films in which she suffers unexpected or unprovoked physical violence

ABOVE AND OPPOSITE Garbo was a 'reflective' actress: violence seldom touched her in her films. *The Kiss* was an exception. As her husband (Anders Randolf) lunges murderously at her young lover (Lew Ayres), Garbo kills her husband, then reports the 'crime' to the police.

LEFT Garbo in control of a more familiar situation.

OVERLEAF, TOP Her old lover, played by Conrad Nagel, gives Garbo a rough time before undertaking her defence.

OVERLEAF, BOTTOM When love, not law, is the subject, the note is tender.

beyond her control. As Charles Affron points out, Garbo is an actress of reflection, not action.

By the time *The Kiss* was premièred, most of the Hollywood stars had taken – and successfully passed – their 'sound' tests. (John Gilbert, the most notable casualty of the talkies, provoked laugher less because of the quality of his light tenor voice than because of an audience's embarrassment at hearing, for the first time, a grown man panting out his love audibly on the screen.) The MGM archives reveal a desire to get Garbo into talking pictures as soon as possible. The studio badly wanted her to be in *Hollywood Revue*, the showcase film in which the rest of their star roster proved they were not natural mutes but could sing, dance and move the lips with sound coming out. But there was one inescapable snag. A memo of 24 October 1930 refers to it: 'We would have had the right to use any of her poses [a legal term for screen image] including her spoken dialogue during her present contract in the *Revue*. However, we are checkmated by Paragraph 17 of her contract which provides that she shall be starred or co-starred; but if co-starred, with a male star only.' Everyone in *Hollywood Revue* was, more or less, a co-star; but the contract-breaker was that a few of the co-stars Garbo would have had to accept were female. The memo continued: 'For your information, Garbo's present contract is still a "silent"' one as she has never signed an agreement to talk. In this respect, she is the one exception in our stock company. The question of her signing was discussed with the advent of sound pictures, but she declined to sign, giving as her reason, as I recall it, lack of confidence in the English tongue.'

What persuaded her to change her mind? Partly inevitability: *The Kiss*, the last film to be shot wholly silent at MGM, is also generally considered to mark the official end of the silent era. Had she not talked, Garbo would have had no employment. And partly Louis B. Mayer's promise that if she made a talkie version of *Anna Christie* in English, he would let Jacques Feyder direct an export version in German, a language she felt more at home with. Mayer also promised to let her work on the German adaptation, along with John Loder's Austrian wife. Garbo liked Feyder, who directed like a more disciplined Stiller; his habit of never crying 'Cut', but instead waving his handkerchief before the camera lens, was an eccentricity that appealed to her. She was promised that her friends Salka Viertel, wife of the German director Berthold Viertel, an intimate of Garbo's and a screenwriter of most of her talkies, and William Sorensen would have roles in the German *Anna Christie*. But first, she must talk in English. She talked. 'Gimme a visky, ginger ale on the side an' don' be stingy, babee,' are the first words heard from her as Eugene O'Neill's dour, man-hating Swede-in-America. The pitch is a shade too

OPPOSITE, TOP LEFT When she made *The Kiss*, Garbo was just twenty-four: it was her tenth film for MGM.

OPPOSITE, TOP RIGHT AND BELOW Directed by Jacques Feyder and photographed by Garbo's technical 'watchdog', William Daniels, the film featured a dramatic courtroom sequence. Conrad Nagel won the case, and his client.

ABOVE Beside a heavily soundproofed camera, photographer William Daniels watches sympathetically as director Clarence Brown and Garbo face the test of talk in *Anna Christie*.

high, the delivery flat, the vocal performance sounds superimposed on a self-consciously down-at-heel woman of the streets. But the *tones* are captivating. 'Her voice', wrote Richard Watts Jr., 'is revealed as a deep, husky, throaty contralto that possesses every bit of that fabulous, poetic glamor that has made this distant Swedish lady the outstanding actress of the motion picture world.'

To hold a dialogue with her public imposed a tremendous emotional strain on Garbo. We are fortunate to possess William Sorensen's eye-witness account of that fateful day she took her voice test. She had telephoned him at 2.00 a.m., and commanded him to come over.

We sat in the living-room and talked about trivial matters. Then, before either of us had realized it, the clock had struck six and a few minutes later the two of us were on our way to the studio. Suddenly it occurred to me she must have stage fright, though she didn't betray herself with a word. I did not say anything either, but just stared straight ahead. Then I heard a voice from underneath the rug beside me in the car. Instead of a rich, deep timbre, I heard the moving plaint of a little girl. 'Oh, Soren, I feel like an unborn child just now.' . . . Awaiting Garbo in her dressing room were Alma, her coloured maid, and Billy, her beauty expert. . . . On that morning their faces showed acute apprehension. I almost expected Alma to break into a wailing Negro spiritual, but Garbo would have none of this Doomsday atmosphere. Her manner had again changed and now she was gay and light-hearted about the whole thing. 'You must go now, Soren,' she told me. 'But please stay in the studio, so we can have lunch together later on.' Just before noon, Garbo called me up to her dressing-room. . . . 'Well, it wasn't really so bad,' she said, 'though I became a little scared when I heard my own voice. . . . I almost jumped out my chair when I heard those lines played back to me . . . but you should have seen how the others reacted. Alma makes a dramatic gesture towards her forehead and appeals to the Lord. Billy gets hysterics and runs out. Some of those tough boys on the set start clearing their throats. [Clarence] Brown [who directed the 'English' *Anna Christie*] comes up, gives me a big kiss and says "Wonderful, Greta!". After that the sound engineer signals to the mixing-room "OK for sound".'[19]

According to Sorensen, Garbo first saw the picture at a downtown cinema the day after its première and, an intonation or two apart, which she suffered in silence, 'she seemed fairly pleased'.

As a child, Garbo had a high-pitched voice. She was obviously well aware, when she returned to Sweden in 1928, that within months she would have to confront the problem of talking in English on the screen. Friends believe it was then she consciously decided that a deep voice carried more authority, and re-modelled her tones on those of the actress Naima Wifstrand whose voice betrayed her Lapland origins (like Garbo's mother) and was not typical of the fashionable Stockholm intonation. Garbo kept Wifstrand company and, as Wifstrand spoke English

TOP AND LEFT By delaying her talkie début until microphones were more sensitive and mobile, Garbo eased her transition into the new era . . . but apprehension still shows.

OPPOSITE, TOP Having henceforth to hold a dialogue with her public on the soundtrack seemed to intensify Garbo's wish to withdraw physically from them elsewhere.

OPPOSITE, BOTTOM Garbo so admired her co-star Marie Dressler's acting in their *Anna Christie* scenes that she sent a bouquet to the veteran player.

OVERLEAF 'I feel like an unborn child just now,' Garbo confessed shortly before shooting her first sound scene.

CHARLES BICKFORD ~ GRETA GARBO ~ GEORGE MARION IN 'ANNA CHRISTIE'

much better than Garbo at that time, Garbo's English had deeper intonations than her Swedish. In her next few talkies, Garbo is to be heard altering her speaking tone quite considerably, retaining Wifstrand's trick of lingering on certain vowel sounds and giving quite ordinary phrases a resonance that awakens strange chords of feeling (Garbo was an excellent and sometimes unconscious mimic). Her voice made other changes in her art. Screenwriters quickly learned to recruit the complex resonances to build up a mood. Garbo's utterances, unlike those of other stars who merely delivered plot points, had the quality of fatefulness, which explains, perhaps, why her talkies grow more and more saturated with vocal pessimism and lugubrious soothsaying.

Garbo's second talkie, *Romance* (22 August 1930), caused hearts to flutter less anxiously in the MGM legal department. M. E. Greenwood, in his memorandum to Mayer of October 1930, added: 'Since Garbo [refused to sign an agreement to talk] we have let the matter ride because, in the opinion of Loeb, Walker, Loeb, by her talking in *Anna Christie* and *Romance* she has construed talking as part of her contract. They feel that if she refused to talk now, we would have the same rights as though the talking provision was in her contract. Furthermore, it is to her interest to talk.' Apart from hearing the vocal conjuring trick that makes Swedish-accented English into a plausibly Italianate sing-song, there is little else of interest in *Romance* which cast Garbo as Rita Cavallini, a flirtatious opera diva, who almost, but not quite, seduces a young curate away from parish and innocence. Gavin Gordon's air of virginity causes Garbo's worldliness to look as if it is suffocating him. Flesh and the Curate was no match for Flesh and the Devil. This was one occasion on which Garbo worked none of the magic on her leading man about which Marie Dressler, her co-star in *Anna Christie*, once shrewdly observed: 'Greta works almost to the point of exhaustion, and her capacity for work is contagious. The fact is, an actor must put forth every last ounce of effort, every minute of his working time, or his role will fall short miserably in comparison to Greta's uniformly splendid work. There are several actors, for this very reason, who have risen to great heights when playing opposite Garbo, only to fall back to their natural levels when appearing in other casts.' Garbo admired Dressler's work beside her enough to send her flowers (yellow chrysanthemums); but the older actress, while flattered, did not soften her focus: '[Otherwise] I have never known her exhibit a lively interest in anything, except once when I [*sic*] suggested the life story of Christina, Queen of Sweden, as a splendid Garbo vehicle. She was really enthusiastic about that: but

OPPOSITE, TOP As Eugene O'Neill's man-hating Swede, Garbo's thawing protestation to Charles Bickford, 'I love you, and I haven't ever loved a man before', was hardly convincing; but her neurotic intensity compelled attention.

OPPOSITE, BOTTOM Hirschfeld's caricature seemed to signify how sound had humanized a screen goddess.

TOP It was back to glamour for her second talkie, *Romance*.

RIGHT 'Like a very round sketch . . . for *Camille*' is how her performance as the *diva* in *Romance* has been described. But Gavin Gordon, though ardent, was no Armand.

OVERLEAF Her wardrobe in *Romance* was one of her most extravagant.

except on that one occasion, she always seems totally uninterested in her surroundings, even a trifle bored.'[20]

Another co-star in several films, Lionel Barrymore, saw the remoteness in a different light: '... her unpretentiousness was so extreme that it amounted almost to a malady. She appeared and disappeared as silently as a wraith. She ignored the grace notes of "Good morning" or "Good night". She was either consumed by the gem-like flame of her art, or was merely bashful. ... She is so diffident that her psychology is comparable to the terror of a gun-shy bird-dog.'[21]

Around this time, the early 1930s, one senses a sizeable increase in Garbo's restlessness, her inability to settle, or to concentrate on anything outside that charmed state induced in her by the camera. She moved again, to 1717 San Vincente Boulevard, sheltered ever more deeply now behind dark cypresses. As well as feeling physically displaced, she was suffering a typical bout of indecisiveness on another score. As far back as 1927, she had said she wanted to become a permanent resident in America. If she married an American, said a studio memo (were they thinking of Gilbert?), she would become one: but this solution was not put to her. Now she had an additional spur: taxation. In 1928 she had had to consent to MGM witholding half her weekly salary – then $2,500 – until the five per cent levied on the pay of all non-resident aliens had been collected. In 1930, she was approaching $4,000 a week; what had been irksome was now unacceptable. By 12 March 1930, she wanted to become a permanent resident alien 'and wanted it quickly', said Charles Green in a memo to F. L. Hendrickson, head of MGM's contracts department. Extraordinary corporate weight seems to have been lent to her desire, for Green said in a letter dated 2 November 1930, to J. Robert Rubin, 'She really cannot go from the status of a temporary visitor to that of a permanent resident alien or make a citizenship application.' But he added he was even then 'trying to work something out ... with the co-operation of Washington'. That 'something' was an amendment to the immigration laws that would put Garbo, and others of her kind, in a special class! But the next year, 1931, she apparently changed her mind again – at any rate, she reported she had lost or mislaid her passport.

Her next film was an insipid romance entitled, wishfully perhaps, *Inspiration* (6 February 1931), about an artist's model ('I am just a nice young woman,' Garbo says, adding with the candour of the coming Camille, 'not too young, not too nice') who falls in love with a budding diplomat played by Robert Montgomery and then deserts him rather than nip his promise. After that came *Susan Lenox: Her Fall and Rise* (15 October 1931) whose main distinction was being banned by the British censor on the grounds of the *novel's* notoriety – the author who had written the book in 1917 had been shot by a crank in protest against his male chauvinist attitudes – and then passed with 125 feet of material deleted from it and the proviso that the title be changed. (It was, in England, to *The Rise of Helga*.) The fact that Garbo is silent all through the first scene, virtually immobile as her uncle sells her into marriage, gives the film

OPPOSITE With her new fluffed-out hair-style in *Inspiration*, Garbo returned to playing the 'loose woman' redeemed by love.

RIGHT Garbo's male leads like Robert Montgomery in *Inspiration* were a poor match for her in her early talkies.

561-131

an old-fashioned silent-era quality rapidly belied when Garbo, sheltering in Clark Gable's forest cabin, returns a marvellously apprehensive 'Yes' when asked if she is a girl. As Richard Corliss remarks, 'She knows what men do to girls.' Gable, minus his he-man's moustache at this early moment in his career, is otherwise in full command of a male situation. 'Coffee?' he asks. 'Caviar? . . . A little port to revive you?' 'Caviar,' moans Garbo, making it sound the very food of love. Cecil Beaton was in Hollywood at this time and described Garbo, at the end of the day's work, leaving the sound stage for her dressing room and 'marching forth as if to the gallows'. He shrewdly gauged the respective muscle power that the star and the studio could impose on each other. 'In many ways Garbo is in a position to, and does, dictate to the directors of her films, but in regard to the plots she plays, they are adamant. They know the financial success of Garbo as a vamp.'

For her fifteenth MGM film she played one of history's greatest vamps – *Mata Hari* (31 December 1931). The British censor, polled protectively by MGM before shooting began, stated that the actual execution of the notorious Javanese-Dutch spy for the German Secret

ABOVE Clark Gable was one screen lover able to hold his own with Garbo in *Susan Lenox: Her Fall and Rise*.

LEFT The Hollywood 'morality code' was now restricting Garbo's display of passion. But in proximity to a bed, her unexpressed desires were unmistakable.

OPPOSITE In Gable's grip, Garbo is for once the submissive partner.

Service must not be shown on the screen – though when it came to the point, much more trouble was precipitated by a scene that seemed to show Garbo's power over Ramon Novarro to be more absolute than that of the Virgin Mary on his bedroom ikon. But in all other worldly matters, the famous purgative presence of Garbo redeemed both Mata Hari and the story from doing more than skirt the circuit of sinfulness – she went to her execution 'purified' by an accompanying squad of nuns, but otherwise much as Cecil Beaton had seen her quit work. It is perhaps her most trance-like performance. The sequence most people remember is one of the weirdly angular heroine in Oriental costume insinuating herself with a swivel of the hips round the huge Eastern idol which looks about to embrace her lasciviously, and finishing the dance with a discreetly masked strip, back to the lens. There are grounds for thinking some, if not all, of this dance may be by a stand-in. Garbo's employers made use of look-alikes to save their expensive star the small chores of lighting rehearsals, etc., but also for certain scenes Garbo jibbed at doing. Geraldine

OPPOSITE, LEFT In *Mata Hari* she performed an exotic temple dance that turned the barbaric god into a many-limbed partner.

OPPOSITE, RIGHT Garbo's headgear in *Mata Hari* was as exotic as her role as a First World War spy, and more eye-catching.

ABOVE Staircases were favoured meeting places for lovers in Garbo films. Ramon Novarro encounters her in *Mata Hari*, while George Fitzmaurice gives directions and (extreme left) William Daniels, at the camera, waits like another kind of lover.

RIGHT The seductress's power, which proved more potent than the Virgin's, made censorship trouble in England for this scene.

124 de Vorak (or Dvorak) substituted for Garbo in the operatic scenes in *Romance* (where she was said to have sung for her as well), in the snow scenes of *Love*, in the car crash of *A Woman of Affairs* (though the actual crash is a badly done model shot), and, when the studio policy required it, even attended premières posing as Garbo. As late as 1941, just as Garbo's last film, *Two-Faced Woman*, was going into production, for which she had to dance a hot Latin rumba called the chicachoca, its casting director cabled a cabaret artist in New York: 'Am looking for Garbo double who is excellent rumba dancer. Remember you well for your impersonation and appearance. But would appreciate you informing me as to your dancing ability, esp. rumba.' (It is not recorded whether the woman was used or not; her name, by one of those freakish coincidences, was Elizabeth Taylor-Martin.) It is worth mentioning that MGM retained numerous rights to double or dub 'the acts, poses, plays and appearances' of Garbo and also her voice in censorship disputes, hazardous acts, long shots, process shots, her failure or refusal or neglect to comply with obligations, her inability to perform due to the need of special knowledge, and in all foreign-language versions of her films. (In this respect, hers was a standard star contract.) *Mata Hari* was the first Garbo film to be distributed in a dubbed version.

'No, I am not in love. No, I will never marry. No, I am not to stop playing in movies, they are my life to me. I am happy to have left New York. They are so impolite in New York.' Thus Garbo, caught at LaSalle Street Station,

Chicago, *en route* for Los Angeles in January 1932. Her replies have now the curt desperation of someone head down, teeth gritted, battling the north wind of bitter publicity. Very bitter indeed the following month when Clare Boothe Luce wrote in *Vanity Fair*: 'Selfish, shrewd, ignorant, self-absorbed, whimsical, perverse and innocent, she is the perfect realization of the child left to itself, unhampered and uncontrolled by mature authority.' This is typical of other attacks she suffered at the time. What the media resented was her changing the rules, all to her own advantage. Many stars enjoyed power without responsibility; well and good, that was news. Garbo wanted and got power without visibility; that was bad, that was no news. The talkies had brought a huge new influx of American and foreign Press correspondents to Hollywood, since Hollywood was now America's overseas empire, setting ways of thought, behaviour, dress and living for the civilized world, or, at least, those parts of it with cinema box-offices. Thus Garbo's most miniscule act, by its very rarity, was instantly disseminated and inevitably magnified. Even the day she broke her hitherto inflexible rule about quitting the set at 5.00 p.m. precisely and, as a special favour to the director, worked twenty-five minutes overtime, was flashed around the world by wire service as if some sovereign ruler had granted a general pardon. She complained of being type-cast on-screen while forgetting that she was just as mercilessly type-cast off it, too. She had created a role for herself that she was destined to play to the end of her days.

At least this year, 1932, gave her one of her most popular (although shortest) film roles, as the *prima ballerina* Grusinskaya in *Grand Hotel* (12 April 1932) whose fear of age and failure is temporarily arrested by falling in love with the gentleman thief played by John Barrymore. MGM had bought the film rights to Vicki Baum's novel *Menschen im Hotel* in 1930 for only $13,500 and maximized their bargain by backing the New York stage production to which the cost of the book was charged, and very soon liquidated. Star-laden and plot-surfeited, the film began shooting on 30 December 1931, finished photography on 19 February 1932, completed its retakes by 29 March and was premièred on 12 April – evidence of the fantastic efficiency MGM had attained in this era. But the efficiency concealed manifold difficulties over Garbo's role. Her screen credit, for instance: in such a showcase production including top stars like Joan Crawford, Lionel and John Barrymore, Wallace Beery and Lewis Stone, how could she be given the solo billing stipulated in her contract? The solution: for the first time on the screen, she was billed solely as 'Garbo'. Harry Edington drafted a prudent memo on this to MGM's legal head on 13 February 1932: 'I took this up with Miss G. and she tells me as follows. That the billing is all right as far as she is concerned and doesn't care anything about it. However, I could not get her to sign in the space specified by you. There is no reason for her not to sign, except for the reason, she simply doesn't sign papers.'

LEFT Sigrun Salvason, one of the Garbo look-alikes employed by MGM to stand in for the star. She was found dead in 1934.

OPPOSITE *Grand Hotel* had an all-star cast: (from left) Lewis Stone, Lionel Barrymore, Wallace Beery, Joan Crawford, Garbo, John Barrymore, Jean Hersholt. One of the few occasions when all the stars managed to get together, and virtually the only photo of Garbo and Crawford (who do not meet in the film) on the same set.

More of a headache to MGM at that time than a star who did not sign papers was: who should *they* sign to direct the film? Thalberg wanted Edmund Goulding, a freelance director good at handling actresses. Mayer feared this might mean an emphasis on Garbo and Crawford that would upset the narrative balance. Moreover he feared other things he had heard about Goulding and on 7 July 1931 he cabled Thalberg in New York: 'Schulberg [B. P. Schulberg, then production chief at Paramount] thru with Goulding. Advised picture he made *Night Angel* cost $600,000. His direction so impossible, unbelievable done by sober man. However, you know him. His salary with them $50,000 a picture. He owes them eight weeks without pay, if they keep him. They are waiving that to get rid of him. Not saying you shouldn't take him, but this info. for your guidance. Urge you to act in all matters as if you owned company 100 per cent. Don't agree you should hold back. Close deals whenever you feel it is good for us. You will make mistakes, so will I. We worry together on our mistakes and glory together on our wonderful accomplishments.' Thalberg did not hold back: he hired Goulding for $1,000 a week for a year plus a $28,000 bonus if MGM exercised an option for a second picture. But relations with the independent-minded and touchy director are best reflected in a note on an MGM memo: 'We only made one picture and charged the full $52,000 to *Grand Hotel*.'

MGM had no reason to regret this 'extravagance'. *Grand Hotel* was an instantaneous and huge success and even now remains among the studio's most jealously guarded properties against the inevitable day of its remake. Though Garbo's role is small-ish and intermittent, she dominates it – and this despite a performance in overdrive from Joan Crawford, as the stenographer who uses sex to get ahead. If Crawford provides the film with its melodrama, Garbo endows it with its magic. Admittedly, the notion of her doing a *pas seul* is laughable – fortunately we do not have to see it – but what she plays is what she is, *a star*. More than ever, the scenario borrows from life to thrill audiences with the sense of autobiography when they hear her moan, 'I have never been so tired in my life', or, collapsing on the floor in a flutter of tutu frills and looking more like a drying heron than a dying swan, give vent to the keening, authenticated version of hundreds of on-the-run Press quotes – 'I want to be alone.' As Pauline Kael has written, 'The fatigue and despair seem genuine. . . . If you want to see what screen glamor used to be and what, originally, "stars" were, this is perhaps the best example of all time.'[22] She had lost none of her directness of attack in the love scenes and John Barrymore in her embrace is like an incapacitated swimmer rescued and beached by a lady

ABOVE As the ageing *prima ballerina* in *Grand Hotel*, Garbo actually did speak the famous words, 'I want to be alone'.

OPPOSITE With John Barrymore. Garbo gracefully submitted to the Great Profile's wish that his better side (the left) be featured in their love scenes.

lifeguard. But the very best things are her monologues into the telephone, without Barrymore at the end of the line ever being seen. Being alone in a scene may feed the ego its richest nutrient: but the truth is that it is Garbo's concentration, not egocentricity, we experience. Such is its power that when she croons pathetically, 'My pearls are old', she resembles one of those Japanese connoisseurs of ornamental rocks in the gravel gardens – she seems to see right through to the heart of the mineral.

Speed was essential after *Grand Hotel*, for an MGM legal memo dated March 1932 confirms, 'Our contract with Garbo terminates April 24, 1932. No further options, save for film completion (up to 40 days).' She was immediately rushed into a production of *As You Desire Me* (2 June 1932), as Pirandello's *demi-mondaine* vamp transformed (or diminished, according to how you desire her) into a high-born wife. Its few pleasures are sartorial – Garbo in a clinging black pants suit and a platinum wig, neon-lit, angular and astonishingly hard-featured – or perverse –

OPPOSITE She related to objects so magically that leading men were often not missed. In *Grand Hotel*, Garbo's best love scene was played to a telephone.

ABOVE With Melvyn Douglas in *As You Desire Me*, after he had transformed the slinky nightclub singer (RIGHT) into a long-lost wife. The catsuit was one of her most extraordinary creations, designed (some said) as a mischievous parody of the Dietrich style.

Garbo for once in someone else's masterful grip, that of Erich von Stroheim who bows back her head for a kiss which he implants with the precision of someone using a bomb sight. Thomas Quinn Curtiss recounts, in his biography of von Stroheim, the protectiveness Garbo extended to him by timing her own 'indispositions' to occur on the days when the man who had been so humiliated some years earlier at MGM telephoned her to say he felt too nervous to appear on the set.

On 29 July 1932, two Burns detectives kept guard outside the unmarked door of a state-room aboard the Swedish liner *Gripsholm*. But the besieging Pressmen knew who was inside, even though her name did not figure under any of her familiar aliases on the passenger list. Garbo's contract with MGM had expired in early June; now she was bound for Sweden. Some people thought she would never return and considered it an omen that the film technicians who had viewed her phenomenal career closer at hand than any other mortals had subscribed to buying her a travelling case. In fact it was to be eight months before she returned, and then as a 'permanent resident'.

It is instructive, and occasionally touching, to see just how scrupulously MGM guarded Garbo's image from those who might despoil it and, even worse, from those who might profit from it. The legal ruthlessness evident in the archives argues for a sort of fond jealousy that has passed away with the disappearance of the contract-artist system.

BELOW The transformation of one woman into another in *As You Desire Me* has been 'read' as a metaphor for Garbo's own career from shopgirl to goddess.

RIGHT Erich von Stroheim played the Mauritz Stiller-like figure of a novelist with a possessive and hypnotic influence on Garbo.

On 18 March 1932, for instance, the publicity manager for Gimbels writes an abject apology for accidentally using the term 'Garbo skirts' in an advertisement for the New York store. On 16 May 1932, MGM's legal department writes a lengthy reply to a citizen of Havana, Cuba, who had drawn their attention to an advertisement for 'Biuty [*sic*] Powder' allegedly sponsored by Garbo. ('Never missing from my boudoir. . . . When I use it after my bath, I experience the sensation of a career.') Solemnly, the studio answers: 'Regarding the use of Miss Garbo's name in association with a "prickly heat product", Miss Garbo does not make any such endorsement.' At other times in other places on the globe, a 'Dawn of Hollywood' range of cosmetics has to be hastily revamped to expunge the 'Garbo' and 'Crawford' hues from the morning skies; a play staged in Buenos Aires under the title *I Am Greta Garbo* has to drop its claim 'as Miss Garbo cannot appear for others'; the manufacturer of Peter Pan Coats who wishes to express his devotion to the star by 'dedicating' one to her draws the blunt reply, 'Miss Garbo is not in this country and it will be impossible for you to send her any coat.' There are limits, though. The trademark 'Garbo' had caused a flurry of panic when the vigilant New York office discovered it on the patents list in connection with a garbage unit. But a cable from Culver City to J. Robert Rubin restores the equilibrium: 'It seems . . . it would be fairly hard to stop the word "Garbo" in connection with a refuse container. . . . It does not seem anyone is going to confuse the two.'

Of course there was good reason for this solicitude. Garbo was a sizeable part of MGM's corporate profit – and an even bigger piece of its prestige. But very few people at this time knew how high a price she had exacted from the studio for things to continue this way; in fact, the contents of the contract she had signed three weeks before she sailed for Sweden have not been made public knowledge till now. They are probably unprecedented in the history of MGM, a studio with a reputation for paying its stars their worth (that 'worth' being capable of adjustment under pressure), but not otherwise giving them access to other means of profit or independence. Garbo's new contract would have caused an insurrection had it been published: for it was nothing less than an agreement to set up a personal production company for her inside the MGM organization. In twenty-two pages it spelled out an amazing relationship between MGM and Canyon Productions 'for the services of Greta Garbo'. So essential was it to fall in with Garbo's wishes that the contract did not even have a time limit: it was to continue long enough for the production of two films starring her. She had the right to designate the date she desired to report for work, giving only sixty days' notice. The only provisos: notice as to the first film must be given before 6 May 1933 and work must begin on it before 6 July. She must give notice as to the second not less than six months nor more than ten months after completing the first. The first film might be produced 'at such place or places in Europe or the British Isles, as we may designate'; the second, at MGM, Culver City, or elsewhere 'as we may designate' – a precaution, possibly, against the studio's never-ending anxiety that Garbo, for some reason or another, might be denied re-entry facilities. Then came her terms of compensation. They were regal: $250,000 for each film. On signing the contract, $100,000 down paid to Canyon Productions; another $30,000 on reporting for work, then $15,000 a week for the next four weeks; the balance of $60,000 to be held in escrow and paid over, with interest, on completion.

But this was far from the extent of the powers granted her. A memo to Mayer from Hendrickson, dated 4 February 1933, states: 'Prior to commencement of production of each photoplay we [are] to submit names of two directors and Garbo has the right to select one. . . .' If she rejected both, or failed to designate either, MGM could pick its own man from the tendered names. But if so-and-so 'was unavailable or unobtainable on reasonable terms or shall not actually perform services as director or if, after commencement of services, we deem such services unsatisfactory and remove him from production of [the] photoplay, his successor [is] to be selected or designated in the same manner as above.' Garbo had a veto over him if MGM wished him to make the second film, too. She had the right to have submitted in advance the names of 'actors and/or actresses whom we intend casting for other principal roles of each respective photoplay, not exceeding four roles per photoplay. Within 72 hours after such submission, she [is] to deliver to us her approval or rejection of persons submitted.' Similar terms as those applied to the directors were extended to cover re-selection contingencies. (It is noteworthy that Garbo claimed no similar powers of approval over her screenwriters, though seven were to labour on *Queen Christina*, seventeen on *Marie Walewska* and ten on *Ninotchka*.) The first film under this queenly arrangement could not have been more apt: it was *Queen Christina*. Others to follow included such suggestions as *Sun of St Moritz*, *Congai*, *Thais* (the Athenian courtesan), *Joan of Arc*, *Three Weeks* and *The Painted Veil*. Here, the choice was MGM's.

What is notable about this arrangement – besides its unprecedented nature – is that no time limit was set for

completing either film; and apart from the May and July deadlines, it was left to Garbo to say when she wanted to begin the first. MGM thought sixty days' notice sufficient, a time scale that will make today's producers blench with fright. Presumably everyone had been so anxious to conclude the agreement before Garbo left America that vagueness had been almost a priority. But memos flew between Mayer and the legal department early in 1933 constructing scenarios based on the inherent risks of the contract. When the call came and Harry Edington notified the studio that Garbo would be ready for work on 15 May 1933, a memo dated 10 April spelled out the awesome consequences: '. . . we should actually start rehearsing or photography on date and if we do not and if she is so minded [a phrase that must have caused a corporate catch of breath] she would have the right to terminate the entire contract and collect $250,000 for the first picture. Starting on that date merely to say we had started and then postponing to a later date would not constitute a compliance with the intent of the contract.' Edington's letter contained even more alarming news. 'She would like to do the second production with only three or four weeks' rest in between.' This was a reversal with a vengeance – hitherto she had been noted for delaying rather than accelerating the arrival of new films and for demanding generous periods of recuperation. A legal hand has noted: 'L.B. [Mayer] said he couldn't promise this, but might work out after she gets here. George Cohen [a Beverly Hills attorney who helped draw up the contract] to talk to Edington and advise us.' Cohen, in an internal MGM memo dated 19 April 1933, appeared now to be regretting the vagueness. No time limit was set for completing the production 'but the intent was that after commencing production we could not postpone for an unusual or indefinite period. If the production

happened to be similar to *Rasputin*, where the exigencies . . . lengthened the production period, she would nevertheless complete the picture. In short, we were to exercise good faith. . . .' A slightly ominous note chills the last paragraph of this memo addressed to 'Mr Mayer and Mr Mannix' (Thalberg's health had collapsed and while convalescing in Europe he was stripped of his production chief title: he returned to a studio split into numerous 'independent' producers responsible to Mayer). It read: 'George Cohen further feels that, notwithstanding the contract ambiguity, there is no question but that she could prove the intent as briefly outlined above.'

Meanwhile, the object of all this intramural anxiety was living in a one-bedroom Stockholm apartment, sunbathing, swimming and taking cross-country hikes with a friend, Countess Wachtmeister, an aristocrat and distant relative of Sorensen's with a Garbo-esque liking for the strenuous outdoor life. She was at sea, on a slow freighter bound for San Diego, coaching herself in the wiles of the self-willed seventeenth-century queen she was to play, when the first of the submissive suggestions on direction and casting arrived by cable. Dated 29 March 1933, it proposed as director either Robert Z. Leonard (who had done *Susan Lenox*) or Edmund Goulding. Garbo had seventy-two hours to deliberate, but took only a day. 'Goulding. Regards. Garbo' snapped the cable sent to 'Loumayer, L.A., Calif.' Mayer was as prompt in replying, on 31 March, with a tantalizing alternative: 'Think there is opportunity of getting Lubitsch. Understood your first preference. Advise if so and will try borrow from Paramount.' Garbo cabled 1 April, 'Prefer Lubitsch. Also happy for Goulding.' A pause indicates the ensuing wheeling and dealing in Hollywood; then on 12 April, Mayer cabled, 'Goulding not available, [Rouben] Mamoulian not on reasonable terms.' (Mamoulian director of *Applause*, *City Lights* and *Dr Jekyll and Mr Hyde* was then the current boy wonder of Hollywood.) Lubitsch proved to be busy preparing *Design for Living* and either could not, or would not, abandon this seductive project even for Garbo. Mayer re-submitted Robert Z. Leonard, and added the ever faithful Clarence Brown. Other possibilities canvassed were Jack Conway, Sam Wood, even Josef von Sternberg whose own version of royal history, *The Scarlet Empress* with Marlene Dietrich as Catherine the Great, was to be shot at Paramount at the same time. Mamoulian either adjusted his fee or, more likely, MGM accepted his terms, for on 17 May Garbo wired, 'Approve Mamoulian.'

She had landed on a permanent resident's visa seventeen days earlier and been met by Salka Viertel with a copy of the *Queen Christina* script. On 2 August, she approved 'as principal possibilities' Laurence Olivier, Ian Keith, Lewis Stone and Reginald Owen. In the film Owen played one of Christina's generals and her abortive suitor, Keith the Queen's lover, Lewis Stone the Court Chancellor, and Olivier was to have been the Spanish Ambassador who captivates her and precipitates her abdication. How Olivier lost the role will always remain a cause for argument. The

'Approve Mamoulian,' Garbo cabled MGM, as the studio prepared *Queen Christina*. By now powerful enough to give orders, she remained a willing instrument in the hands of the few she trusted, such as director Rouben Mamoulian, here temporarily occupying John Gilbert's seat on the set of the snowbound inn.

MGM files do not take us much further into Garbo's reasons for rejecting him; what they do is evince the sizeable embarrassment even a major studio can suffer at the whim of a star backed by a cast-iron contract.

Oddly enough, Olivier had been Garbo's suggestion. She had seen him in RKO's romantic weepie *Westward Passage* as an effervescently irresponsible young writer whose looks strongly recalled John Gilbert's in his silent heyday. On this evidence alone, she must have 'approved' him, for Benny Thau, the film's producer, cabled Sam Eckman at MGM's London office: 'Laurence Olivier will call on you for transportation. Please arrange same. We have signed him for Garbo picture, including first-class transportation for himself.' The very first scene they had to shoot together was Christina's meeting at the inn with the Spaniard. Olivier had had misgivings from the first. He realized on first meeting her that she was going to be difficult to know – 'shy as an antelope', was how he put it. To his conversational ploys, she returned monosyllables. The day arrived when they met on the set, Olivier in costume from an earlier take in which Garbo did not appear, Garbo in an off-duty outfit of lounging pyjamas and smoking a cigarette. It was against her nature to rehearse: but she had established an increasingly intimate relationship with Mamoulian and agreed to play a love scene with Olivier to give the director some idea of what the British actor would be like. Olivier explained: 'The director said I was to come forward, grasp Garbo's slender body tenderly, look into her eyes and, in the gesture, awaken the passion within her. . . . I went into my role,

giving it everything I had. But at the touch of my hand Garbo became frigid. I could feel the sudden tautness of her.' They tried again . . . and again. They had a little walk, a smoke and a chat together, anything to establish a rapport. They went into the scene once more. 'Garbo froze up as before.' Realizing that Garbo's attitude would register 'cold', Mamoulian flung down his script, called a halt and bawled in exasperation, 'In Heaven's name, is there any man this woman *will* warm to?'[23] According to Olivier, one of the technicians cried out, jokingly, 'John Gilbert'. Then and there, Mamoulian invited Gilbert to come over and stand in as a means of bringing Garbo up to the required emotional pitch. When all saw the effect on Garbo of Gilbert, now wearing Olivier's costume, what was to have been merely a rehearsal process became a major piece of re-casting. On 15 August 1933, twelve days after filming had begun, Garbo sent a memo to the legal department: 'This is to confirm the approval heretofore given by me that John Gilbert shall be substituted therein, in lieu and instead of Laurence Olivier.' Olivier did not return to Hollywood for six years after this set-back (though when he did it was a different story and his Heathcliff in *Wuthering Heights* revealed how an actor of talent had grown into a dominating screen presence).

ABOVE No mistaking what sold the film. 'GARBO' covers the frontage of New York's Astor Theatre. Even 'Greta' is superfluous.

OPPOSITE 'The idea of a woman in cavalier clothes has a visual aspect that is appealing to her,' Cecil Beaton wrote of Garbo as the Swedish queen travelling, incognita, in male attire.

If this is how the co-starring role with Hollywood's most famous actress was actually cast, then it is unique in production history. Were Garbo and Gilbert in collusion? Gilbert, who died of alcoholic debilitude and a heart attack in 1934, cannot tell; Garbo will not. Mamoulian tends to confirm Olivier's version, while hinting that the studio would have preferred John Barrymore to any contender. Does one detect the hand of Harry Edington, trying to spring a come-back in the most public way for his old client? The most chivalrous explanation is the simplest and perhaps the most likely: that Garbo, in return for the favour Gilbert did her in co-starring her in *Flesh and the Devil*, was simply sending back the elevator for an old flame and a fallen star.

Other terms that Gilbert accepted were less generous: the contract he signed, and from which he sought declaratory relief in court a year later, was for a mere $20,000, a tenth of what he had commanded four years earlier. For the legal department there was the nightmare of the billings. Ian Keith's contract had given him second place to Garbo, but now Gilbert had been signed. 'Other than that,' said a resigned memo from F. L. Hendrickson on 11 October 1933, 'at the time this contract was signed we already had a contract with Laurence Olivier which called for second billing to [Garbo]. Fortunately for us, Olivier did not prove up to the requirements to play the part.' Keith gallantly accepted the situation and agreed to Gilbert's name preceeding his in larger type. Much of film history is writ in similar capitals.

Queen Christina (26 December 1933) is more a commentary on Garbo mythology than a chapter on Swedish history. Its psychological moods are so patently and often

astutely borrowed from hers by, amongst others, her close friend and screenwriter Salka Viertel, that one seriously wonders if the film implanted the seed of abdication in her thoughts. There is one bizarre coincidence. The name which the bisexual monarch took as her male pseudonym in her years of forgotten exile in Rome was 'Count Dohna' – the first role Garbo played in a major feature was as *Gosta Berling*'s Countess Dohna.

The film set the star's public image till the end of her talkie days and her roller-coaster descent into comedy in *Ninotchka*. It is the fabric of a woman's mind that furnishes the intellectual stiffening for the historical fol-de-rol. Some scenes make Garbo, then just twenty-eight, look not only years older but centuries wiser. Such is the moment she quells a mob in mid-rush up the palace staircase to chide her for having a Spanish lover, lectures them on the cares of monarchy and then, as they shuffle out mumbling humble apologies, arches a sardonic eye-brow at their child-like trust in history's text-book simplicities. William Daniels, as usual, does his uncanny lighting job on her face – even inventing a long strip of ground glass which he gradually pulled over his otherwise too-hard wide-angle lens as it closed in on the famous last shot of Garbo, blank-faced as per Mamoulian's instruction ('Think of nothing'), as the queen's boat leaves Sweden forever. But the great set-piece

OPPOSITE A male will in a female container is how some characterized Garbo. In *Queen Christina* (flanked by C. Aubrey Smith and John Gilbert), she lost no chance to fashion a masculine container for her will.

BELOW Sexual ambiguity runs through *Queen Christina*: even the ladies of the court pay homage to a monarch in breeches. With Elizabeth Young and C. Aubrey Smith.

is the bedroom sequence. Mamoulian, with an opera background and knowledge of choreography, commanded, 'Do it to music', importing a metronome to keep Garbo in time as she moves round the room, touching the objects in it as if each were a trysting-place in Eden, while John Gilbert watches in half-amused perplexity. She uses her hands like a divining rod seeking the well-spring of love, caressing the walls, turning the spinning-wheel (and it is an odd bit of bedroom furniture, admittedly) like blind Atropos reaching with her shears to cut the thread of fate, embracing the disturbingly phallic cone of unspun wool, sliding over the bed and pressing her face to the sheets and blankets as if they were her lover's breast, then wading across the huge bed like a snowdrift to press herself up against the bedpost in as near an orgasmic rapture as Hollywood dared come in those days. At which point, as the music stops, she moans, 'I have imagined happiness, but happiness you cannot imagine.' What makes her craft so breathtaking is how she plays the scene simultaneously

RIGHT 'I shall die a bachelor.'

BELOW A regal presence surrounded by male courtiers. With her own production company inside MGM, Garbo, just turning twenty-eight (the same age as Queen Christina), may have felt that life was now aping history.

OPPOSITE, TOP Life did, indeed, take the course of history when, less than ten years later, Garbo followed Queen Christina's path to self-exile.

OPPOSITE, BOTTOM Gilbert and Garbo in the inn scene: 'Entirely un-Swedish . . . utterly insulting to Swedish royalty,' carped the film's historical adviser. He even objected to the fruit they ate.

OVERLEAF *Queen Christina*'s furniture-touching sequence.

140

1 As John Gilbert watches, Garbo moves

2 among the furnishings of the inn bedroom,

5 touching objects like someone seeking

6 the source of love.

9 Gilbert: 'What are you doing?'

10 Garbo: 'Memorizing this room . . . I have imagined happiness,

but happiness you cannot imagine – you must feel it.

12 *The Lord must have felt like this when he created the living world.'*

142   for sorrow as well as joy. The words about preserving her rapture ('In future, in my mind, I shall live a great deal in this world') relay a brooding undertone of someone preparing herself, amidst inexpressible joy, for certain loss and loneliness.

The sequence is all the more marvellous if juxtaposed against the report of the Swedish historical adviser, one Colonel Einhornung, whom MGM, sensitive to possible offence that reigning royalty might take to the portrayal of their ancestors, had employed to vet every detail of script and production. The colonel did so, and his advice was cheerfully ignored by Mamoulian and company. An almost comic irritation shows up in every line of a lengthy document that instructively suggests how prosaic reality was converted into screen myth. 'Even Miss Garbo', the colonel writes, 'pronounces "Oxenstierna" [the Lewis Stone character] in Norwegian, "de la Gardie" in French, and "Helsingborg" in Danish. . . .' Her love affair 'has no historical background. . . . It is a gross insult to Swedish history and Royalty and Swedish womankind to picture the Queen as a "light woman" who goes to bed with a complete stranger after having known him for a few hours. . . .' As for that 'stranger', he goes on, 'the wig that Mr Gilbert wears is entirely too short. . . . Nearly every person in this picture wears too short wigs. . . . Very few of the swords are of the right kind. . . . People of standing never wore light-colored hose. . . . Parliament did not clamor for war, the people were tired of it.' The scene of Christina's levee was particularly affronting. 'I objected strongly – in vain – to having Aage [the C. Aubrey Smith character] in the bedchamber when the Queen dresses, also to his helping her dress.' And what of the film's most celebrated sequence? 'The whole inn scene is entirely un-Swedish. I protested – in vain – against the candles on the tables. As for the bedroom scene . . . I have previously pointed out how utterly insulting this scene is to Swedish Royalty. During most of these scenes, the set was "fenced in", so I do not know what was done. However, when I saw apples, oranges and grapes carried in, I pointed out the impossibility of having them served at the inn, even if it was suggested [the Ambassador] brought them from Spain. He had been travelling for weeks, and, besides, no fruit could be kept edible in the very cold winter climate of Sweden.'

Later in Sweden, running true to form, Garbo deprecated her part in the film, saying she had 'tried to be Swedish . . . but there is no time for art. All that matters is what they call box-office.' But if that was 'all that matters', the studio must have been disappointed too. *Queen Christina* was the first Garbo film to show a sizeable dip in her box-office fortunes, particularly in America where Depression-era filmgoers sought consolation in the peppy sentimentality of Shirley Temple comedies or the hard-boiled optimism of Busby Berkeley routines. Nor did her next film, *The Painted Veil* (7 December 1934), restore her fortunes. 'Main objection', David O. Selznick said in a cable to the studio where he had been made a producer, 'was lack of opportunity Garbo wear clothes and those she wore were terrible.' It is a phlegmatic film, everyone looking exhausted by the heat of the Orient – the least propitious element for Garbo, being utterly alien to her nature – and what one recalls most vividly is her headgear,

'Make your face a perfect blank,' Mamoulian instructed Garbo. Audiences did the work of reading her mind.

the extraordinary 'trowel' hat and her conjuror's ease in winding a towel round her head to form a turban (but then she had posed for hats in the PUB catalogue before her career began). At over a million dollars, *The Painted Veil* was an expensive example of eccentric millinery.

At least her worth to MGM had not depreciated. Her personal production company had been wound up on 12 August 1934, just a year after its creation, in circumstances which suggest that the pending or enacted fiscal legislation of the Roosevelt Administration persuaded Canyon to go into liquidation right away. It had had a contract for Garbo's services for $2,000 a week for five years – thus spreading her tax liability – at 50 per cent of the net profits of *Queen Christina* and *The Painted Veil*. On 23 October 1934, Garbo signed again with MGM – this time for a single picture and at a fee of $275,000!

Garbo at this time was under the strong influence of two women-friends. Mercedes de Acosta was a New York-born socialite of Spanish descent; poetess, authoress of historical plays staged in vanity productions, health-food crank and religious-cult devotee, she led Garbo intellectually through the same pursuits, shared vacations with her, suggested film subjects – *Joan of Arc, The Picture of Dorian Gray* – and generally used life as raw material for conversion into self-romanticizing memoirs eventually published under the typically self-dramatizing title of *Here Lies the Heart*. Salka Viertel had a more concentrated intelligence and a more practical hand in the creation of Garbo's screenplays. Both women leaned by temperament and talent towards the 'large', the 'historical' and the 'European'. Selznick had begged Mrs Viertel to get Garbo to agree to 'a modern subject'. Mrs Viertel, though, favoured a remake of *Anna Karenina*. 'A heavy Russian drama on the heels of so many ponderous similar films!' cried Selznick in horror. It was more than timely, it was essential to attune Garbo to the new public mood. He had sought a modern comedy. Finding none, he suggested a modern drama such as *Dark Victory* which, by good chance, was owned by Jock Whitney who was soon to be his partner. Even better luck, Fredric March, whom the studio wanted as Garbo's co-star, felt he was better in modern-dress stories 'and we are doubly fortunate that the male lead (in *Dark Victory*) is strikingly well suited to Mr March'.

It was all in vain. *Anna Karenina* (30 August 1935) had the consequences Selznick feared for Garbo. It seems dated rather than period. Meticulous costuming and settings representing 1870s St Petersburg are constantly undercut by the posturings of a supporting cast whose reactions to scandal resemble those of vulgar provincials. March is coarse-grained, with a wooden plank of a body which Garbo has to use as a sounding board for her own range of emotions, which are by far the finest things in the film. When Basil Rathbone, as Karenin, orders her to quit their house and abandon their son, Garbo's figure descending the grand staircase slumps concavely with the invisible weight of social ostracism that all the voluble tut-tutting from society matrons cannot match. The drama progresses with staid pageantry between two memorable shots of

In *The Painted Veil*, a 'veil' was one of the few bits of headgear she did *not* wear. Trowel-style, turban and hospital wimple, however, did not relieve the story's dullness. Nor did George Brent.

OVERLEAF, LEFT The opening sequence of *Anna Karenina*.

OVERLEAF, RIGHT The closing sequence of *Anna Karenina*.

146

1 From the start of the film, a fatefulness

2 envelops the doomed lovers, as Vronsky (Fredric March)

3 encounters, emerging from the steam, the woman

4 who will ruin herself for love of him.

5 This sense of destiny

6 now becomes almost tangible in Garbo's films.

1 Destiny at the beginning, doom at the end.

2 As the abandoned Anna sees her lover departing,

3 Garbo's face, almost without moving a muscle,

4 hardens into a suicidal resolution.

5 As the wheels of a shunting train approach,

6 she jumps to her death in a blur of despair.

147

Garbo's face: once appearing out of the locomotive smoke at the beginning; and again illuminated by suicidal despair in the light of another train at the end before she throws herself under it. She does not die – she vanishes, as if she had never been.

On 30 May 1935, she committed herself for two more films at $250,000 each – *Marie Walewska* and *Camille* – with the same approval of directors, players, etc. as before. Clearly, there was no easy escape route from 'history'. If the Hays Office did not approve of Garbo as a courtesan in *Camille*, the studio reserved the right to substitute *Woman of Spain* (probably a version of Merimée's *Carmen*). Garbo now used her regular Swedish vacation as psychological capital to sustain her through a year or so in Hollywood. But on this occasion 'something happened', something still not satisfactorily explained.

The first Mayer heard of the 'illness' that had afflicted Garbo came in a letter to him from Laudy L. Lawrence, head of MGM's Paris office, to whom Garbo had written from her Stockholm address at Klippsgatan 6, asking him to get her brother Sven employment with the film company. She suggested Kr. 15,000 (nearly $4000) for a three-year minimum, a not inconsiderable sum. Lawrence wrote directly to Mayer on 3 December 1935, either as a result of a visit by Sven to him in Paris, or by him to the Gustafsson household in Stockholm. 'Sven is a nice boy, but that is all . . . his health is very bad. Incidentally, the entire family is in bad health, including Garbo. . . . I believe her younger sister died from TB long ago and Sven is in bed a whole lot more than out of it. Garbo is rather seriously ill.' Rumours of Garbo's illness now began

appearing in the international Press, which referred to it as a heavy cold or influenza. It was clearly far more than that. On 8 December 1935, Garbo wrote one of her longest and possibly most intimate letters to Louis B. Mayer. It is also one of the most touching pieces of evidence of how seriously she took her career. She still addressed Mayer as 'Sir', and thanked him for MGM's efforts on her brother's behalf. Then she referred to her own bad health. She had been ill since September, confined to bed almost all the time; but even with the possibility of an operation hanging over her, which she dreaded, her thoughts were on work, and she ended her letter by expressing the hope that her next picture would be done well. The fact that she and MGM had now settled on *Camille* gives the letter an additionally pathetic resonance, and it is an important clue to the authenticity she was to bring to the film's concluding scenes when Camille faces the fact of her approaching death. Garbo's only request was an extra month's recuperation. Mayer cabled her on 10 January 1936 to say he was 'terribly distressed', and to assure her that 'all contract obligations would be suspended for a month'. Five days later, Garbo replied: 'Agreed. Thank you. Feeling better. Greeetings. Garbo.' The return to her customary terseness perhaps indicates the extent of her improvement.

Except for a star-producer like Chaplin, who owned his pictures outright, Garbo was now the highest-paid talent in Hollywood. Her contracts had become intricate series of

ABOVE New York City, January 1937: opening day of *Camille*, and what many consider Garbo's greatest performance.

OPPOSITE With Robert Taylor. No other Garbo film had so many pains taken with its production. Perfection was the aim.

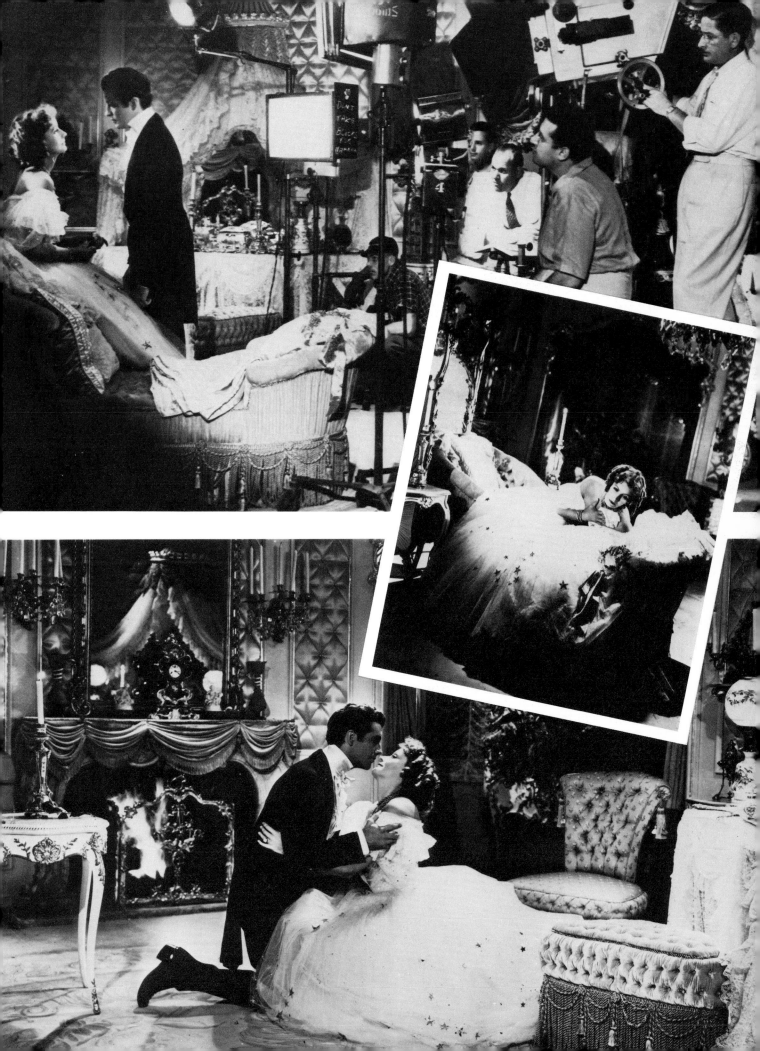

step-by-step approaches to the start-date of production, whereupon she would go on full, munificent salary. Once she had thus 'commenced production', shooting had to begin within a certain date or all kinds of penalties ensued. Nothing better illustrates this than Garbo's offer, out of fondness for Adrian, to appear in his workroom and be fitted with her *Camille* costumes 'without compensation'. Danger here! An MGM memo said, 'We discussed this with George Cohen, who advised against permitting Miss G. to appear for fittings unless an agreement was signed by her under the terms of which she agreed that the two weeks' period would not commence.' (MGM was liable to pay Garbo $10,000 a week for any two weeks 'prior to the time we had planned on starting'. They had planned on starting the two-week period just prior to shooting.) The unnamed memo-writer added his own self-protective marginalia: 'Went to Mr Hyman, who phoned Salka Viertel, who confirmed Garbo's view. Discussed with Mr Thau, who spoke to Mr Hyman, who confirmed his understanding of Garbo's agreement. Permission to attend Adrian was granted.' Very different from the time, just ten years earlier, when she was peremptorily suspended for *refusing* to attend the studios to get her wardrobe for *Flesh and the Devil*. Now her star power and economic muscle, coupled with MGM's infinite cautiousness in handling such volatile substances, endowed a costume-fitting with the minutiae of legal protocol.

Camille began on 29 July 1936. Anxiety to keep shooting on schedule was increased by the star's power. Her contract stipulated that if she was still working after twelve weeks, she must be paid $10,000 average per week or any part thereof. In fact she must be kept on salary till her services, including retakes or additional scenes, were completed. Anxiety did not end with the picture. On 5 November 1936, a memo was circulated bristling with queasy self-interrogations. 'G's contract provided for a rest period of five weeks between pictures. What would happen if we made retakes and then let her go? If we found we wanted to do a retake, what would our position be? If we call her back, does her rest period start all over again? Would it be an advantage to let her go, then make up our minds if we wanted her to do a retake? Would we be any the worse off?'

She was now at the peak of her power and in the prime of her art. What gives *Camille* (22 January 1937) its freshness is the unbroken line of Garbo's performance, and the way she plays against all expectations. For the anticipated capriciousness of the *grande cocotte*, she substitutes a ruthless self-scrutiny that recalls those letters she wrote to her schoolfriends when she was only into her teens.

Films about intelligent women in love are not all that common. It takes actresses of a very special disposition to portray both states plausibly and simultaneously. Greer

TOP With Henry Daniell, one of the few actors who could steal a scene from Garbo.

OPPOSITE, TOP LEFT Her face in *Camille* would often express an acceptance of a tragic destiny.

OPPOSITE, TOP RIGHT Director George Cukor instructs Robert Taylor in how to carry his precious burden.

RIGHT Only studio executives knew how ill Garbo had been before she played Camille.

OPPOSITE, BOTTOM But one critic was right when he said of Camille's death scene that Garbo looked as if she had lain in bed for weeks.

PUBLICITY — SZERELEM

Garson, Katharine Hepburn, Celia Johnson, to name a few of the very few, have managed it at times in their films; Garbo in *Camille* manages it all the time. Her rich protector, played by Henry Daniell (one of the few actors who almost capture a scene from her), is particularly unperceptive when he sneers, 'So much heart and so little sense.' Garbo's Camille is a perfectly balanced equation of heart and head. It is something for a woman as hotly in love as she, on being told by her lover that her courtesan friends do not suit her, to reply, 'Nonsense! They are the only friends I have and I am no better than they are.' She is cool, but, as director George Cukor commented, 'seething underneath'. Cukor noted another thing had matured – her skill at getting more from less. The 'plastique' of her movements he was to recall years later: 'When de Varville [Daniell] makes her pick up [her fan] she makes a remarkable movement, almost like something in a dance, like Isadora [Duncan]. She doesn't kneel to pick it up, she bends sideways in the most natural way.'[24] Most of the time, too, she suggested tuberculosis by dry little clearings of her throat, or even by so slight a gesture as touching her mouth. And when she dies in Robert Taylor's arms, she signals death by opening her eyes – a reversal of expectations so startling that it has had some viewers swearing they have glimpsed the body give up its soul.

Marie Walewska (US title *Conquest*: 4 November 1937) was bound to seem a come-down after *Camille*. The highly fictionalized story of the affair between Napoleon and his aristocratic camp-follower from Poland, it was yet another of those 'large' subjects to which Salka Viertel had helped Garbo become addicted: a fustian role unconcealed by a sumptuous wardrobe, an expensive cast, and that old stand-by, the snow. (If in doubt, bring down the snow, seems the standing instruction to Garbo screenwriters.) 'Are you real or born of a snowdrift?' is thus the unwontedly lyrical enquiry addressed to Marie by Napoleon when first they meet. And winter, too, is for once given amorous preference over spring as the season that brings soldiers home to their women – soldiers of the rank of emperor, anyhow. The extraordinary exchange of memos about the right title for the film (see Filmography) indicates a serious division at MGM over whether they were making an American movie or one aimed at Europeans. When Garbo sailed for Sweden again on 10 December 1937, it was the first time she had left the United States without leaving a signed contract behind: a clear sign of the serious hiatus developing in her career.

But if the world public was less than captivated by Garbo as an emperor's *inamorata*, their curiosity about her relations with another despotic man of his time knew no bounds. Garbo and Leopold Stokowski had met in Hollywood in mid-1937. At fifty-five, Stokowski was twenty-three years older but also a star in his own world – the conductor's podium and the Hollywood musical – and thus there was an 'elective affinity' between a pair who realized that their individual charisma would burn with refreshed incandescence just by reason of their togetherness. They had more down-to-earth tastes in common, of course: each was a crank in the art of living. Stokowski, in mid-age crisis and separating from his wife, was concerned with health – i.e. retaining his youth – and Garbo, always a food faddist, was into that 'yoga and yoghourt' experience that later generations would pursue with even more narcissistic fervour. The two of them were besieged by the international Press when they rented the Villa Cimbrone at Ravello, in March 1938. What the Press imagined was going on inside was one thing; what the gardener later reported was another: a strident Garbo-esque voice drilling Stokowski much as he dealt with his musicians, 'One – Two – Three – Bend! One – Two – Mr Stokowski, you are out of time!' The companionship ran its course: then it simply ran out. It had enhanced each and probably exhausted both.

'My next film will be a comedy.... Will I be allowed to keep my lover in it? Certainly I am hoping so. Don't you think it is high time they let me end a picture happily with a kiss? I do. I seem to have lost so many attractive men in the final scene.' She seemed at her most cheerful and accessible that autumn in Sweden. Her 'romantic' liaison with Stokowski had caused MGM some slight anxiety and they pulled strings to have a re-entry permit arranged before she sailed, so as to avoid the prospect of Immigration asking embarrassing questions. They need not have worried. William Orr, of MGM's New York office, informed the studio on 10 October, three days after Garbo's arrival, that he had talked to the Immigration officer 'before he went in

OPPOSITE, TOP Garbo's next essay in historical doom, *Marie Walewska* (*Conquest* in the USA), was ill-fated in other ways. It co-starred Charles Boyer as Napoleon, but was felt to be top-heavy with period dressing.

OPPOSITE, BOTTOM Garbo, increasingly restless, took a European holiday with conductor Leopold Stokowski. The *paparazzi* pursued them, even into Vatican City, believing a romance was blossoming. But one cartoonist judged the joyless companionship more accurately.

BELOW Garbo's career needed refreshing. In Ernst Lubitsch, she found the director to do it; and in *Ninotchka*, just the film to spoof her own humourless legend.

to see about Garbo's papers. He came out after about fifteen minutes, told me everything was okay, but evidently she had imbued him with some of this secrecy serum, as he refused to tell me anything else.'

On 29 December 1938, Garbo signed a one-picture deal with MGM for $125,000 – a sizeable drop in price from the $275,000 she was able to demand for *Anna Karenina*. *Ninotchka* (9 November 1939) did the last thing left to do to the Garbo myth – it debunked it. 'GARBO LAUGHS' was truly all the film needed to publicize a story that spoofed her style of humourless brush-off by converting it into an amorous crush. 'Do you want to be alone, Comrade?' asks one of the comic commissars. 'No,' she replies – the anti-myth in monosyllable. She gives heart to Lubitsch's

heartlessness, too. Melvyn Douglas teases her with being jealous of the more soignée White Russian Grand Duchess (played by Ina Claire, the widow of John Gilbert!). Garbo appears to pull back shyly ten feet from him. Then those amazing eyelashes of hers flick down, like a row of power

OPPOSITE 'Garbo laughs!' was all that was needed to publicize *Ninotchka*. The cause of her mirth: Melvyn Douglas, evoking a response from Garbo's dour commissar only when he is so carried away by his own joke-telling that he falls off his restaurant chair.

ABOVE A transformed Ninotchka meets the White Russian Grand Duchess. For Garbo, it was also an encounter with Ina Claire, widow of her old love John Gilbert.

156 switches, and she utters a tiny, tremulous, girlish admission of 'Uh-huh.' That is all – 'Uh-huh.' But it is like a pebble dropped into a deep abyss of feeling. Not the sound it sends back, but the depth it signifies, is the impressive bit of emotional evidence.

Garbo's sense of taste was as intuitive as her sense of acting: and both were self-protective when necessary. Maurice Zolotow in his Billy Wilder biography revealingly disclosed the one time Lubitsch deviated from the screenplay to adjust a line for a performer – for Garbo. Orating against the capitalist railroad system, Ninotchka deplored that the first-class carriages had velvet chairs, the second-class, calf-leather seats, the third-class, wooden benches. 'We Communists, we will change this from the bottom up,' she was to cry. Garbo objected that the word 'bottom' had coarse overtones. Lubitsch deleted it, 'not so much to placate Garbo, as because he agreed that it was a vulgarism which was out of character'.[25]

Garbo's switch to screen comedy was accompanied by a lightening in her temperament and an off-screen attraction to the eupeptic Gayelord Hauser, the health guru and now her willing guide to the life spiritual and the body temporal. He had something in common with all the men who briefly took control (or so they thought) of Garbo's directionless life: a sense of showmanship which connected with Mauritz Stiller's early flamboyant example. Hauser answered people's need for flattery, reassurance and control. He moved Garbo into the international set, changing her social ways as well as her eating habits, and thus set her on the lines she was to follow in the decades ahead. He put her in her place without apology – which was welcomed by a woman who had not found or made a place for herself. In short, he directed Garbo's attitude to herself in much the same way as subtle and sympathetic moviemakers had directed her in the playing of a character.

The war was a severe blow to Garbo. Within weeks, MGM had lost the major part of the European box-office; at that time about forty per cent of the company's revenues came from abroad. The new movie for which she signed a contract on 20 November 1940, giving her $150,000, was therefore deliberately tailored to secure the profits of the home market. And Garbo had to be 'tailored', too. Her hair was bobbed, her curves emphasized by a more revealing wardrobe. She was to play an outdoor girl in scenes showing her swimming and ski-ing. Indoors, on the dance floor, she was to be an oomph-girl, one step away from the lonely soldier's pin-up. But the scene in *Two-Faced Woman* (31 December 1941) that caused Garbo most concern was the one in the pool. George Cukor, hired to direct at $3,500 a week, tried to set her mind at rest by calling for help from a woman they both admired, Katharine Hepburn. Cukor wrote to her in New York on 10

TOP Her performance in *Ninotchka* was widely acclaimed; one leading critic called it 'a joyous, subtly shaded and utterly enchanting portrayal.'

RIGHT AND OPPOSITE *Two-Faced Woman* attempted a radical re-jigging of Garbo's screen personality. It laid stress on her 'new' likes and aptitudes which included swimming (coached by director George Cukor, in shirt sleeves). MGM's promotion sheet did not lack suggestions, either.

OVERLEAF Garbo doing the chicachoca rumba was one of *Two-Faced Woman*'s boosted attractions. She faced up gamely to transformation into an 'oomph' girl. In these remarkably candid photos, she is being rehearsed by choreographer Robert Alton. His verdict: 'She has a marvellous sense of timing.'

GARBO'S VERSATILITY HAS BIG PROMOTION VALUE!

April 1941, asking her to help out another great artist. The problem was the bathing suit Garbo had to wear. Choosing any wardrobe was an exhausting task for her; now the decisive moment when she would have to expose her full figure in a close-fitting garment utterly defeated her. Cukor remembered that Hepburn had had a bathing suit designed by the *couturière* Valentina – who later, along with her husband George Schlee, was to become one of Garbo's intimates – and he begged her to air-mail it to the Coast without delay (not that it would be used in the film, simply to allow Garbo to see the type and try it on). Cukor had made several films with Hepburn, including *The Philadelphia Story* the year before, and he ended on a waggish note by reminding her that he had brought her back from oblivion! Apparently Hepburn's swim-suit persuaded Garbo to do the scene.

No one was prepared for the furore of criticism that fell on this inept but innocuous comedy about a wife who teaches her errant husband a lesson in fidelity by pretending to be her twin sister and seducing him. Garbo played both roles. 'Un-Christian towards marriage ... impudently suggestive ... dangerous to public morals ... salacious costumes' (no, not the swimming-costume, the dance-floor low-cut gown) – all this from the Roman Catholic Church's National Legion of Decency, deploring a plot which required a man to appear to flirt with his wife's sister. MGM spent $14,000 shooting an extra scene in which Douglas is shown to have gone into the 'affaire' with his eyes open, thus nullifying the comic point. But nothing could soften the critics' blows. 'Its wickedness lies in its vandalism,' Cecelia Ager wrote in *P.M.*, 'it makes Garbo a clown, a buffoon, a monkey on a stick.' It is true the film gave Garbo no room, no scene, no moment to project her knowledge (and forgiveness) of human nature. It is a clockwork sex comedy – i.e. a comedy in which no one ever

has sex – about mistaken identities. Doris Day and Rock Hudson inherited its formula in the 1950s.

For a woman who never rehearsed the emotions of a scene on a film set, but only the mechanics, this was a film that was all mechanics and no emotions. There was probably another reason why the film failed – one that was forecast by the prescient Elinor Glyn eight years earlier. 'If Greta Garbo were to play two parts in the same talkie, no matter how marvellous everyone found her acting, that magic fascination which she puts forth would immediately go. The public unconsciously would know it was "art" and all illusion of her mysterious personality would vanish.'[26] It was all too true. The illusion had vanished; yet it was not even 'art' that remained. Around the same time Adrian, who had wrapped Garbo in costumes more palpable yet just as exotic as that mystery, left the studio to become a freelance couturier. 'When the glamour ends for Garbo, it ends for me.' He was saying much the same thing as Mme. Glyn. An upset and bewildered Garbo had made plans to go on a Mexican vacation just before the première, but William Orr talked her out of it by advising her that 'for patriotic reasons' a trip to a foreign country was imprudent – Pearl Harbor had just been bombed and America was in the war. Garbo had said, in what was to be her last appearance on the screen, 'In this harsh new world there is no place for me anymore.' That, too, was like a line from her autobiography.

Garbo's last film hit censorship trouble because of its story of a girl who marries a New York tycoon (played by Melvyn Douglas), then has to put on the glamour and romance him afresh (BELOW) by pretending to be her *soignée* twin sister and so outwit his seductive old flame (played by Constance Bennett, CENTRE). Catholic censors asserted that adultery did not mix with kith and kin.

Garbo in the late 1950s: 'I'm sort of drifting.'

ALONE AT LAST

THE PUBLIC may not have welcomed *Two-Faced Woman*; but inside MGM Garbo continued to be held in awe and apprehension. The policy of apartness which she had maintained over twenty years, out of genuine shyness as well as policy, did not rebound vindictively on her once her career was seen to be faltering. One woman employee, still at the studio in 1979, recalls the 'early warning' put out to the wardrobe department where she was a young assistant in 1942. Miss Garbo would be paying a visit the next day. All staff not directly occupied with her should keep discreetly in the background and try not to catch her eye. Though there was no love lost between them, Louis B. Mayer still prized her; even if he had not, he would have wished to deny her services to rival studios. It is noteworthy that although Garbo was now a free agent, able to go where opportunities offered, she showed no in-clination to quit the protection of a studio that had been her workplace and surrogate 'home' since she set foot in America. She still wanted to make pictures. The trouble was, what kind of pictures did she want to make? She had had a box-office set-back, though MGM would always insist that, in the long run, *Two-Faced Woman* did not lose money; and this increased an uncertainty that had already been felt in the need to 'Americanize' the Garbo image. It was also perceptible in the endless title-changes that some of her recent films had undergone right up to the time of opening (see Filmography). What manner of expectations did a modern audience now bring to a Garbo production? Did they want a contemporary Garbo or a period one, a comic muse or a tragic one, a love story or a love-lost story?

Both parties re-considered their position and meantime the studio did not relax the vigilance that had always protected its human assets. They were even more solicitous when Garbo asked for their help – as she now did – than when she had the contractual whip-hand over them. In 1942, when she feared Sweden's neutrality might not be respected by the Axis, she decided to bring her sister-in-law and niece over to America. A bulky studio file discloses the tireless efforts that the MGM executives made to ensure their safe and probably preferential arrival in America via the Argentine. Part of their considerateness involved producing guarantees that the refugees would be cared for by a fit and proper person – to wit, Garbo. This produced some nice ironies. Louis B. Mayer found himself writing to the State Department, on 30 March 1942, to testify that 'Miss Garbo is a person of fine character and a thoroughly reliable and responsible individual.' Eddie Mannix wrote in the same vein. Salka Viertel was asked to sponsor Garbo's relatives; but she regretted she did not feel able to do so, as she had 'signed in' so many, mainly Jewish, refugees during the previous year. So Bernie Hyman, of Loew's Inc., MGM's parent company, obliged.

Evidence of Garbo's good standing with the banks was also obligatory – and the documents throw a minor but interesting sidelight on her affairs at this date. The assistant manager of one Hollywood bank she had used since December 1937 reported that 'the balance averages five figures at all times'. It was very satisfactory, he added piously, that he had never been approached for credit 'and we have reason to believe that she has a very substantial net worth'. Another bank in Los Angeles where she had opened an account in 1933 testified that the average balance for the previous three years had been $122,000. Garbo had a peasant's canniness about keeping money: her wishes never exceeded her needs, and her needs were small. In most of the houses she inhabited, for instance, she used only a few rooms and kept the others locked and empty. She had exported a sizeable chunk of her earnings to Sweden, ever since a brush with the 1929 bank failures prompted her to act on the principle of divide and prosper. In later times she was able to develop a keen sense for the experts whose advice would help her preserve the value of her savings. She invested in property in New York and Los Angeles from 1933 onwards – and today is said to own sizeable chunks of Beverly Hills' richest shopping thoroughfare, Rodeo Drive. One of her Swedish benefactors, Max Gumpel, a property magnate with a flamboyant liking for stage and screen folk, had helped her with the purchase of her country house outside Stockholm, which she sold at the outbreak of war for a satisfactory profit. Her family and relatives were no drain on her resources: they lived modestly, in seclusion, and her mother died in California. There is no point – quite apart from the impertinence – in trying to guess how much Garbo is worth today. Reports have mentioned a trust fund set up to provide her with $200,000 a year after she reached the age of fifty (in 1956). Friends like the shipping magnate Aristotle Onassis and at least one de Rothschild were well placed to protect her from the ravages of inflation. At a time when she did not know much about art, she knew a good investment; a friend who visited her Hollywood home in 1948 counted a Rouault, a Modigliani, a Bonnard and two Renoirs, one of them probably a landscape she had bought at public auction in New York a few years earlier for a 'mere' $8,000. Even in 1942 she was a multi-millionaire.

The war neither touched her financially not stirred her passionately; her own nature precluded the sort of war-work that the stars got up. Apart from her desire to assassinate Hitler, already alluded to, she is not on record as making any less bloodthirsty political gestures. It had not always been so. Members of the Lincoln Brigade who had fought against Franco in the Spanish Civil War were surprised, on disbanding, to be entertained to a brunch at Farmers Market, Los Angeles, where an inquisitive Garbo appeared and questioned them about their baptism in the anti-Fascist battle lines. By World War II, she had lost her curiosity. William Orr made tentative enquiries in 1943 as

to whether she would record a message in Swedish, for broadcasting overseas, expressing America's esteem for her neutral homeland. The request was Government-inspired. No matter: it got nowhere. Garbo's resistance to being 'used', even for the war effort, was inflexible. A much touted story, current in recent times, that she worked as a secret agent for the Allies, spying on Swedes of dubious loyalty, has everything going for it as romantic fiction, but not a single supportive fact.

But by now MGM had fixed on a new subject for her: a war film. It was fortunate for Garbo, perhaps, that the Soviet Union's anti-Nazi policy opened up a wider casting horizon than might have been the case if Hitler had stuck by Stalin. This was reflected in the title of the proposed film: *The Girl from Leningrad*. An early synopsis suggests that Garbo was to be cast as a Russian resistance fighter. On 20 December 1942, she signed an agreement to make the picture and collected $70,000 – another $80,000 would be paid her as work on it was completed. It was the same price she had commanded for *Two-Faced Woman*, though a sizeable drop from her peak figure of $275,000 (or more, if one counts overage pay). It was the last time she signed an MGM film agreement. For, although Greta Garbo certainly did not appreciate it at the time, she had already embarked, as decisively as Queen Christina into self-exile, on that long, long retirement which has now lasted nearly forty years or twice the span of her working lifetime. The proposed film was never made – she found the script 'depressing' – and she was never to make another film. To be 'at liberty' was now to be at a loss.

It is certain Garbo never imagined things would turn out that way. She had no intention of retirement; but the failure of *Two-Faced Woman* made her exceptionally, obsessively careful about committing herself to a picture. Suggestions were made in plenty; she analysed each one with the suspiciousness she had long applied to life in general. Like life, so with a script – Garbo was not willing to take a risk on it. Looking back on the possibilities channelled towards her, by one indirect means or another, what strikes one with depressing repetitiousness is how 'safe' most of them were. It was hard to wean a star like her off her self-protective pattern.

She seriously considered a story casting her as a woman skipper in the Norwegian merchant navy. But mostly the parts she pondered were status roles, ones already enhanced by history or a literary pedigree: Madame Curie, George Sand, Sarah Bernhardt, Joan of Arc, a remake of *Inspiration*, her 1931 talkie, with Montgomery Clift in the Robert Montgomery role. Gabriel Pascal invited her over to England at the end of the war to be Shaw's St Joan – 'the idea of women in cavalier clothes has a visual aspect that is appealing to her,' Cecil Beaton wrote in his diary at the time – but the costly failure of *Caesar and Cleopatra* snapped Pascal's credit line to his backers.

Raising money for a Garbo film for the first time began to present a considerable financial hazard even for those with a good track record. Independent producers like Walter Wanger or David Selznick, cut loose from the cash-boxes of the major studios, had to perform juggling feats to get the budget together. Selznick, the reluctant producer of *Anna Karenina*, sent a note to the agent Leland Hayward, whom Garbo had approached, saying that at the present time, 1947, she was not regarded as a drawing card any longer by anyone in the industry; but as public taste had improved,

he personally believed 'she would be accepted today as never before, and could be an even bigger star'.[27] While he was at MGM, he had bought *The Paradine Case* especially for Garbo, and the role of the heroine with a taste for the poison bottle was written with her in mind. It was proposed to her again; she turned it down again. About the same time RKO approached her with *I Remember Mama* and were rewarded with the telegram, 'No murderesses, no mamas.'

Matters were not assisted by the maddening uncertainties of never quite knowing where one was with Garbo from one minute to the next. Even contact with her was like wartime espionage. Typically, she still did not keep a lawyer on permanent retainer, but hired one as and when she needed him. Producers would have to appeal to her through influential intermediaries, which generally meant Salka Viertel, a woman with her own strongly developed ideas about what suited Garbo. One winces at some of the missed chances, though maybe not *My Cousin Rachel*, which she rejected – 'I could never be Cornish' – after Cukor had dashed to England to try and secure it from Daphne du Maurier. But Cecil Beaton reminds us she was offered Blanche's role in *A Streetcar Named Desire* and turned it down with the infuriating admission, 'I could never be an involved and complicated person. I'm too direct and too masculine: I couldn't bear to tell lies . . . like that girl in the play.'[28] She did jump at the chance to play Elizabeth of Austria in Cocteau's *L'aigle a deux têtes* for Alexander Korda. But that collapsed because of Korda's prior commitment to Eileen Herlie; the consolation prize of Mme. Ranevska in Chekhov's *The Cherry Orchard* was unacceptable.

It is possible to see why Garbo was so choosy. She operated on instinct; Chekhov's reputation meant nothing to her: 'It's not exciting, it's not for me,' she told Beaton. That was that. But inevitably her lack of enthusiasm conspired with her downbeat disposition to produce the

OPPOSITE Men who could use their worldly power to protect Garbo became her companions after she left MGM. With Aristotle Onassis in Monaco in the 1950s.

BELOW Garbo, in a group that includes Onassis and George Schlee, greeting Gracie Fields during a call at Capri by the Greek millionaire's yacht, *Christina*.

feeling of bad omens: each time she had really wanted a part, ill luck intervened. Such 'luck' was actually no more than the commonplace accidents or irreconcilable circumstances which are inherent in movie-making the world over. But it did not appear so to Garbo: she was coming to feel she would *never* make another film. No longer did she have direct connections with a studio that in the past had *made* things happen for her; she also had no talent for making things happen by herself. How *could* she have developed such talent? Her disposition was permeated with the impregnable attitude of not caring; it had won her many a battle at the old studio. Now even when she tried to move events along positively, in her favour, she handicapped herself. Nature got the better of opportunity.

One particularly promising opportunity occurred in 1949. For a reported first payment 'on account' of $50,000, Walter Wanger, producer of *Queen Christina*, had tapped her enthusiasm for the Duchess de Langeais in the Balzac novel about the nobly-born lady who jilts her lover to enter a convent and assume the veil. Garbo was to be directed by Max Ophuls, who would surely have safeguarded her image and perhaps even enhanced a countenance on which the hair-lines of age and the tautness of inner tension were imprinted. She was approaching forty-five. James Mason was to co-star and James Wong Howe actually shot some costume tests, the only known footage of Garbo in colour (and now said to be 'mislaid'). But an essential part of the

LA4) LOS ANGELES, Feb.9--GRETA BECOMES CITIZEN--Actress Greta Garbo signs for her citizenship certificate in Federal court here today where she took her final oath and became a U.S. citizen. The ... Swede, heavily veiled, hurried away without ... (ap30ws)1951

production was backing by the Italian publisher and entrepreneur Mario Rizzoli: it was to be an Italo–American co-production. For this, Wanger deemed Garbo's presence in Rome essential to clinch the deal with her own unique magnetism.

An eyewitness has left a vivid impression of Garbo's sojourn in the Eternal City. Inevitably it is an exterior one, but it conveys tersely the problems that accompanied any Garbo project, as well as recalling the highly public visibility with which she was henceforth increasingly to cloak her public peregrinations. She had travelled under the *nom de voyage* of Harriet Brown, the one she had at last fixed on from a sheaf of alternatives employed over the decades. ('Miss Brown,' Ivor Novello once said to her, 'now we know each other better, may I call you "Harriet"?') 'There is a swish of revolving doors, and a figure that looks like a devotee of some less austere monastic order emerges. An enormous straw hat covers four-fifths of the face; there are sun glasses unseen beneath the brim. There is a loose one-piece dress, caught at the middle with a simple girdle. On the feet there are sandals. It is Miss "Harriet Brown". In one stride she is inside the car. A man following takes one stride, and is beside her. The door slams. The high-powered roadster roars off, followed by three cars, two jeeps, and a motor-cycle. . . . Back to the hotel. Miss "Harriet Brown" sweeps through the swing-doors and, like a shot from a gun, is in the lift, leaving the great bouquet of flowers from her Italian producer . . . where it has been since the morning, on the porter's desk.'[29]

Garbo's landmark mysteriousness – her straw hat soon became as conspicuous a feature of Rome as St Peter's cupola – did not help the project along. Quite the reverse, it was believed. Her frustrating inaccessibility and virtual inscrutability – she was said to have received her producers in a sitting-room shrouded against the daylight, and herself additionally veiled, as if the persona of the convent Duchess had already descended on her – exhausted the patience of the not overly equable Italians. Perhaps, too, they saw the production problems that might arise out of Garbo's self-protective aura. In its day, inside a Hollywood studio, this had worked to Garbo's advantage: but that day was yesterday, movies had moved out of the studio and neo-realism was opening every aspect of life in post-war Europe to inspection on the screen. The deal fell apart. 'It was agonizing and Garbo felt completely humiliated,' George Cukor recalled.[30] 'I have no plans,' she told a reporter in 1950, uncharacteristically confiding, 'I'm sort of drifting.'

By now, too, she had drifted out of direct mention in the voluminous MGM archives. It is a curiously touching sensation when one discovers that the studio with which her fame and fortune were inextricably linked has begun referring to her in the past tense, the way a devoted secretary would deal with the estate of an exacting but regretted employer, now deceased.

The public record from now on always seems to be catching Garbo in transition. Her restlessness had been largely tempered by having Hollywood as her anchor. Even so, her constant move from house to house showed a near-neurotic tendency to wander inside the compound confines. She was not a recluse in the sense that she stayed put for long; she became a recluse, paradoxically, every time she went out in public. She once said she liked travelling because you were alone, you did not have to meet people.

The ideal state for Garbo would have been to be alone – i.e. unrecognized – in a crowd.

Not that she was even now exactly 'alone'. It would be better to say that she was often accompanied, though never permanently attached. 'What I can never understand', William Sorensen wrote in 1955, 'is why she has never exerted these powers [to captivate men] with any seriousness, outside the range of the cameras. Any mortal being with whom she came in contact would have succumbed to her potent powers of attraction. . . . Yet she has decided instead on the lonely life in which she lets her enormous sex appeal lie dormant.'[31] Cecil Beaton is one of the few who got the opportunity to ask Garbo to marry him, and remembered the moment well enough to set it down later.

OPPOSITE, TOP Other less illustrious companions were there to use their physical power to shield a legend from the pursuing publicity.

OPPOSITE, BOTTOM At long last an American citizen. On 9 February 1951, Greta Garbo signed a certificate in a Los Angeles court, took an oath of allegiance, and became a United States citizen. Then, showing she had not abandoned other native-born traits, she hurried away without comment.

BELOW A Cecil Beaton portrait taken in April 1946. 'By degrees,' he wrote, 'she started to assume all sorts of poses and many changes of mood. The artist in her suddenly came into flower.'

OVERLEAF One of Beaton's most eloquent studies, also taken in the 1940s.

Garbo answered Beaton: 'But we would never be able to get along together and, besides, you wouldn't like to see me in the mornings in an old man's pyjamas.' – 'I would be wearing an old man's pyjamas, too. And I think we *would* get along well together – unless my whistling in the bathroom got on your nerves.' – 'You're being very superficial: one doesn't plan one's life on other people's bathroom habits. Besides, you'd worry about my being so gloomy and sad.' – 'Oh no – you'd have to worry about why I was so happy, and you'd be the reason.' – 'It's a funny thing, but I don't let anyone except you touch my vertebrae – they so easily get out of place.'[32]

This exchange is worth recalling for other reasons than its momentous if unrealized possibilities. For one thing, it recalls, in an eerie fashion, the deft flippancies of that scene in *Two-Faced Woman* where Melvyn Douglas offers Garbo 'a star, a carpet to the moon, cream from the Milky Way'. She turns this down flat, too: 'What would I do with a star? A carpet to the moon, it's too bulky. Cream from the Milky Way, it's too fattening.' To talk to Garbo in any vein – tender, sad, flirtatious, lugubrious – is to find oneself talking film-script dialogue, with the slightly disconcerting qualification that now there is no film to go with the dialogue. Once heard, the sound of her voice – that 'arckscentte', as Beaton characterized (and transcribed) its enduring huskiness – explains why her utterances, be they ever so trivial, have a vibrancy that sometimes seems more lively than the phlegmatic personality accompanying them. Garbo brings out people's mynah-bird compulsion to mimic her – in doing so, they keep her alive in public memory, if not view. Most of the anecdotes about her depend on *hearing* her. One woman newspaper columnist appeared unexpectedly at a party and was thrilled to discover she had gatecrashed Garbo. She was also so egoistic that she did all the talking. 'I must tell my friends I've met you,' she cried on leaving. Came the growl: 'Be sure to tell them it was by arckscident.'

Instructive, too, is the story of Garbo visiting Gertrude Stein's friend, Alice B. Toklas, who asked if she would like to see her patroness's collection of paintings. The lights were turned on above each frame; and without moving from her seat in the centre of the room, Garbo swivelled her gaze from canvas to canvas, making no comment till she had completed the *tour d'horizon* of an incomparable collection and then saying, with total finality, 'Thank-you.' When she had gone, Miss Toklas was equally terse. 'Mademoiselle Hamlet,' she remarked.

More recently, the White House implored a friend of Garbo's to intercede with her and persuade her to attend the banquet that President Kennedy was giving in honour of Queen Elizabeth II. Garbo, instantly on her guard, asked, 'What are you getting me into?' Then she said she had nothing to wear (her standard excuse for not doing anything she does not want to do). The friend persisted: they could go out and choose an evening gown; it would not take long, ten minutes. Garbo reportedly considered this none too subtle pitch to her notorious dislike of dressing up, then said in tones of stern rebuke, 'What do you mean, "ten minutes"? Do you think one gets to meet a queen every day?' Needless to say, the meeting did not take place.

Many people, even friends, have found her on-again, off-again relationship tedious in the extreme, but pardoned her the way one pardons tiresome invalids – their incapacity redeems their importunate natures. Some who privately alleged that Garbo had no talent for friendship nevertheless admitted they forgot any resentment the minute they were in her company. A notoriously 'difficult' person can create a charmed circle just on account of his or her perverse nature. This is certainly true of Garbo.

A few, a very few, remained unimpressed. 'I'm afraid I didn't catch the name,' one would-be wit and non-fan said to her. She was not amused. Conversation with her usually leads back to her. She has no store of small-talk, except among intimates: which is to say, her talk emphasizes her emotional feelings, not her opinions. This of course came in useful for fending off the Press. 'Has any romance come into your life while abroad?' She replied, 'Isn't life always full of romance?' But although this is typical of the way she deflects enquiries, it also characterizes her preference for the abstract over the personal. The playwright Robert E. Sherwood was fond of telling how he had once spent two whole hours alone with Garbo, cloistered in the bedroom of a friend's apartment during an inconveniently crowded party. 'And what did the two of you do together?' he was asked. 'We talked.' – 'About what?' – 'About . . . peace.' Direct questions about herself are her pet aversion. Guests indelicate (or inexperienced) enough to begin quizzing her speedily lose her. If she ever alluded to Hollywood, which was increasingly rarely as years and domicile distanced her from it, it was always 'that place' or simply 'in other times'.

Very occasionally, Garbo would be taken by the notion to see one or other of her old films, which meant applying to the cinemathèques, for by the 1950s all but a few of her films had passed out of general circulation. Hollywood at that time had not begun trading with the enemy, so Garbo could not see her past coming up nightly in the late, late slots on the television networks. Her movies had become museum pieces; she, a living fossil. Even facing a lens held by the most professional of friends was an ordeal that had to be conquered by degrees. When Beaton took a new passport photograph of her in 1946 – after her timorous and indirect hints that she needed one – she faced his Rolleflex 'as if it were a firing squad' and only gradually did the artist in her 'come into flower'. Eleven years later, the neurosis was even stronger. Anthony Beauchamp, the portrait photographer, wooed her professionally for ten nights running before she consented to pose for five (and five only) colour shots; 'and after each picture I had practically to tie her to a chair to get another.'

Her brother Sven died around this time; her nearest relatives were Sven's natural son (also named Sven) and his daughter Gray. Sven Gustafsson lives in Stockholm at the time of writing. A charming man in his sixties, as open to serious enquirers as his aunt remains closed to them, his warmth and modest pride in the relationship by all accounts reflect the more equable, outgoing temperament of Garbo's sister Alva whose early death, at the start of her own very promising film career, has already been referred to. Sven Gustafsson has not met his aunt since the mid-1930s; he writes to her, but preserves an understandable discreetness about her replies, if any. His half-sister Gray was mentioned in *The New York Times* in May 1955, when she was at Yale Law School and engaged to marry a

OPPOSITE Three more Beaton photographs, two from the 1940s and the other (top right) taken in 1959. Garbo's concern for her health did not extend to cutting out cigarettes.

physician. The report made no mention of Greta Garbo. She need have no fear that her remaining kin exploit their relationship.

Garbo's closer 'family' has been composed of the contracting circle of the wealthy and influential people able to extend to her the protection of their connections and the privacy that money can still buy for those with enough of it. Many of these people are or were 'stars' in their own small exclusive world: the late Aristotle Onassis and Sir Cecil Beaton, Sam Spiegel, Baron Eric de Rothschild, Irwin Shaw, Peter Viertel and his wife Deborah Kerr. They have easily adapted their ways to the demanding, 'extra-special' nature of their friend and guest. Garbo regards such people as trustworthy in the sense that they, too, rely on others to keep confidences about them and their way of life. More practically, they are, in the best sense of the word, 'fixers', able to do for Garbo what her own horror of dealing with strangers has always made terrifying – 'arranging' relations with the outside world, at ports of call, with Customs and Immigration, and ensuring that expensive modes of transport (yachts, private aircraft, chauffeured limousines on 24-hour call) will always be in place for the secluded

pick-up or the quick get-away. Incapable of good management herself, Garbo has always appreciated it in others.

This is the clue to her long and close relationship with the man who dominated the later stretches of her off-screen life, George Schlee, a financier resident in New York, where he also managed his wife Valentina's *maison de couture*. Known by others, envious perhaps of the access to Garbo he enjoyed, as 'the little man', Schlee's origins, like Mauritz Stiller's, were Russian. He also had Stiller's self-possessed abruptness, a manner of bidding other people do his will which worked because he always assumed they would; and, like Stiller, he enjoyed the good things in life to which Garbo, by no means indifferent to comforts others provided, had been introduced by Stiller.

OPPOSITE, TOP AND ABOVE With Schlee in 1956: a handy coat cloaks the fugitive.

OPPOSITE, BOTTOM Growth of a persecution complex: George Schlee orders off unwanted publicity, 1949.

RIGHT Garbo grabs her companion's hat, c. 1950, but forgets about the treacherous wall mirror.

this always rang a Pavlovian knell in Garbo's mind. She was 'alone' again and now in her sixties, a time of life when one's own mortality is calculable – and, in her case, bleakly ironic, since immortality was already hers, and unwanted.

Paradoxically, she might have found it psychologically easier to make a screen come-back in these years than in earlier decades. Her face had now set undisguisably into the lines of early old age. She would not have had to confront the emotionally daunting competition with the recent image of herself which a return to the screen at an earlier age would have entailed. One would have missed – one did miss! – the middle part of Garbo's life and art, but would gratefully have settled for her 'third act'. Ingmar Bergman had asked her to appear in *The Silence* in 1963. It would have been her first Swedish-speaking role. The two talked a couple of hours together: but it led to nothing. Bergman's friends believe that Garbo sensed she would have had to place herself totally at the service of her director's own obsessive interior feelings. 'Auteurship' was a quality (officially) unknown in her days of Hollywood stardom. It was a feature of the new post-war world of filmmaking where the director was 'superstar' – for a time, anyhow. That made Garbo instinctively apprehensive: she preferred a script to a psyche.

The last stir created by rumours of her impending return was as recent as 1976, when Luchino Visconti, then mentally adding stars to the cast in order to whet his bankers' confidence in a project to film Proust's *A la recherche du temps perdu*, offered her the role of the Queen of Naples (yes, another Royal!), the sixty-ish exile whose arm sustains Baron de Charlus when his morals come

She had met him and his wife when Gayelord Hauser, attempting to smarten her up as part of her spiritual tonic, took her along to Valentina's salon. The Schlees were one of the reasons why she disposed of the lease she had taken in a New York hotel when she made that city her home after the war. She sold the apartment to Greer Garson, and moved into the same co-operative apartment block as the Schlees on East 52nd Street, with a view (by squinting sideways, anyhow) of the East River that may recall the Stockholm Sound for her, if the light is right. The Schlees and Garbo – the women sometimes creating an eerie impression of parallax vision by dressing in look-alike creations designed by Valentina – were often seen around town. In the summer, Garbo moved to Schlee's French residence, Le Roc, at Cap d'Ail. Schlee now 'directed' Garbo's affairs for her, the way some of her other men friends had done in the 1930s; and his disciplining decisiveness was something she relished, as long as it posed no threat of exploiting her for her fame, or tried to tie her down contractually or emotionally.

Schlee's sudden death from heart failure in 1964, when he and Garbo were staying at the Crillon, in Paris, was cause for Garbo to panic and flee to friends, leaving Valentina to take care of the obsequies. For this, Garbo received some censure from the media, which must have caused her great grief; and it was reported that, while they continued to live in the same apartment block, she and Valentina rarely saw much of each other after Schlee's death. Its unexpectedness must have seemed a fateful repetition of her first mentor Mauritz Stiller's sudden slip into mortality forty-six years before. Events like

under attack at the Verdurins' reception. But Visconti could not raise the money (and would not use any of his own), so the project languished – and Garbo felt fate had again rebuffed her.

She now passed her days in New York in the relatively unvarying, aimless routine that many a retired lady of modest means and no celebrity becomes addicted to by necessity, not choice. She would emerge at about ten o'clock from her carefully undesignated apartment – until recently her bell had only the initial 'G' beside it – dressed in a dark cape-type coat, face-hiding hat and sometimes trousers (now no longer an unusual sight). Walking briskly enough for her age, but increasingly with a slight stoop, she would perambulate the bigger stores and small antique shops. Antiques were a taste she had caught from Stiller back in the *Gosta Berling* days when both of them toured Sweden's towns and villages in Stiller's Kissel roadster, digging out genuine antiques for props in the films. Now she seldom bought any item.

Her closest friends were beginning to die off, or be stricken in various ways. Beaton went in 1980. Salka Viertel died in 1978, curtailing Garbo's annual stay at the Swiss mountain resort of Klosters, where those who rose early enough used to see her, on the balcony of the chalet apartment she rented, indefatigably doing her calisthenics. Her lifelong concern with her own health now tended to turn into a vague hypochondria. In 1979 she saw Nils Asther, then in his early eighties and working briskly as an amateur artist whose satirically anti-religious subjects were on view in a Stockholm gallery when this writer was there in the same year. It was assumed Garbo might join Asther in the residential colony of small chalets for the

ailing or elderly not far from Stockholm. So far, she has not repatriated herself: nor gives any sign of it.

Garbo as a person has never crossed the generations. People who got to know her well were generally of an age with her. Unlike such stars as Dietrich, Gish, Swanson, even Mae West, she has not been anxious to make contact with those not born under her stardom. Young people in any case seldom get a chance to meet her unless they are talents in their own field of art, or the children or companions of her current host. On the screen, though, it is a different story. Suddenly, in the early 1960s, a great revival occurred in the public popularity of Garbo's pictures. When they were shown on Italian television cinema audiences slumped alarmingly. The lesson was quickly and profitably drawn by MGM which put them back into the cinemas. In London, people of every age, and particularly the young, flocked to see her in a repertory season of half-a-dozen of her best-known talkies at a West End cinema. In the days of Technicolor and wide screen, Garbo still had the power to draw people into her aura. Nowadays there is a retrospective of her movies happening

OPPOSITE, TOP A tragic-visaged Garbo arrives at Kennedy Airport, New York, 10 July 1964. A few hours earlier, the body of her long-time escort George Schlee had been flown home from Paris following a fatal heart attack.

ABOVE A walk in a wintry Swedish park: Garbo (centre right) and her friend, Countess Bernadotte.

LEFT All alone on a Swedish lake . . . except for the lurking photographer.

nearly every week somewhere in the world; they are the staple entertainment of television, and not always in the late, late zone.

This is more than a nostalgic phenomenon. Garbo's own fugitive appearances in public, as she is inevitably caught in transit by some loitering *paparazzo*, looking white and grim, like someone suffering from a nervous condition and not a chosen state of grace, have preserved interest in her and her legend, willy nilly, for a vastly longer span of time than any woman in her mid-seventies could have hoped for. Indeed, her public persona – if this is not a contradiction about someone so reclusive – has become a token of stardom for people who have never seen a Garbo film. The astonishing thing is that the world's respect for her enormous talent has never buttressed her confidence in herself; she has always been dissatisfied with her own work. A virus of this kind is more usually caught in Europe than Hollywood and there can be no doubt from whom Garbo caught the infection. Her encounter with Mauritz Stiller was a transformation scene in more ways than simply changing the direction of her career, from stage to screen. It altered her nature as well as refining her talents – and it caged both inside another person's aspirations for her.

The object of the *paparazzi*'s pursuit was also at the mercy of the world's cartoonists. Sotero's caricature was part of *Two-Faced Woman*'s promotional campaign designed to 'humanize' Garbo. The Major drawing bears her autograph.

Greta

"ICH STEH' IM REGEN UND WARTE
UND WARTE - - -"

Greta Gustafsson had quite a different temperament: she made friends, she played actively, she worked hard in the public, almost promiscuous atmosphere of a backstreet barber's, she was an avid theatre-goer and movie fan with a crush on some of the stars of her day, she willingly sent herself up in publicity films for the store she worked in, and romped about unselfconsciously in a bathing costume in a slapstick farce. And then she met Stiller. Suddenly, with only a change-of-name declaration at the Ministry of Justice to signal the transformation, Greta is gone and in her place is Garbo, serious about her art, made to suffer endlessly for it, self-critical to an unbearable degree, never satisfied with her work and painfully conscious about her 'self'.

Had Garbo stayed in Europe and never followed Stiller and her destiny to America, the chances are that she would be no happier today. But she would probably have found more opportunities for the kind of work he had taught her to think worthy of herself. Such artistic satisfactions were supplied more abundantly by the European mode of movie-making: the one that Hollywood traditionally bought up, brought over and converted into its own commercial image. Somehow we never think of Garbo as 'American' (in the well-ordered library of Stockholm's cinematheque, she is still listed as a Swedish star). Garbo

was never indoctrinated in Hollywood's show-business tradition. Her ambitions (such as they were) were all against the exploitation that is at the hard heart of that devouring system. Her natural apathy protected her against feeling the loss of things like money, fame and popularity which most other stars cared about obsessively – an obsession manipulated ceaselessly by those who owned them. Garbo never developed the anxiety about not being in work which frequently compelled her peers to accept standards that demeaned their talents as long as continued exposure to the fans fed their egos. Such temperamental fortitude unfortunately made it fatally easy for Garbo to drift out of her career – though not her legend. When she expressed a regret – and expressed it in action by absenting herself from the studio for long periods of time and at some financial sacrifice – it was invariably over not being put in a worthier picture. She frequently remarked to her friends that she had never once gone to a preview and come away

ABOVE Caricaturists' pens were easier to bear than the obtrusive camera lens. Garbo slams the door on a New York photographer, 1949.

OPPOSITE A brisk trudge along the beach in the mid-1950s while staying with her Swedish friends, Count and Countess Wachtmeister.

were on her and then she let thought and feeling work in collusion with light and shade and the unique architecture of her features – and there emerged not just a single aspect of her being (which is the most that the majority of stars can summon up for inspection on demand) but a multiplicity. If anyone doubts that Garbo 'contained multitudes', let them simply look at the pictures in this book, never mind the images that move on the screen.

From the minute she reached Hollywood, Garbo worked for only one company, Metro-Goldwyn-Mayer, and in a very real sense she is the purest art-object that the production system of her time has left us. This book's central section has outlined the enormous care that MGM took of her; or, if you prefer it, the undeniable self-interest underlying such corporate parentage. It has also suggested the corresponding use that a star such as Garbo made of her power in order to enhance her art; or, if again you prefer it, to aggrandize her bargaining status. When all the charges and counter-charges that have been made about the demeaning nature of the star system are examined, and sometimes proven, one inescapable conclusion remains. Garbo and Metro were not just good for each other – they were essential. Without the studio, Garbo drifted purposelessly into inactivity, though happily not into oblivion. In her fifteen-year reign at MGM she was sustained by a system that, however much she hated it, however grudgingly it capitulated to the demands she made on it (and the unique way in which she made those demands), was one that ultimately enriched her and itself – and us. To be put into films that were unworthy of her was a hazard that faced every star. And there was no guarantee that if she had had total freedom of choice, she would have chosen any better than Mayer, Thalberg and the other people at MGM. Later on, when she had total freedom, after she had left the studio, she did not exercise her choice at all!

Chaplin and Garbo are the cinema's greatest stars. They were products of a particular conjuncture of time, place and temperamental opportunity: things that will never recur in the cinema on the same scale with the same impact. Unlike Chaplin, however, Garbo never could have attained – and would certainly never have enjoyed – total entrepreneurial control over every aspect of a movie (including the box-office). But, like Chaplin, she imposed herself on an industrial system and made it work for her uniqueness. Even that word 'uniqueness' is misleading, for inside the confines of popular entertainment she was able to suggest the whole complexity of human nature. It was a marvellous gift. The accidental inheritance of birth and upbringing brought it to Greta Garbo; Mauritz Stiller transformed it into art; Metro-Goldwyn-Mayer helped refine and record it; the cinema has preserved it. If the source of Garbo's art finally eludes us, that is not really a cause for wonder or sadness. It is part of a wider complexity than the way any individual succeeds in combining her personality and opportunities with the age she lives in. 'There is a mystery in you,' John Gilbert says to her in *Queen Christina*. And the answer she returns must be our consolation, too. 'Is there not in every human being?'

feeling happy. She always felt she had fallen short of the perfection which Stiller had drilled her to achieve.

If one feels robbed of enrichment when thinking of the films that, for one reason or another, Greta Garbo did *not* make, we at least have a powerful consolation she was denied. We have only to throw a beam of light on a blank screen and there she is, the essential Garbo, exposing her 'self' to the camera with a candour and amplitude she refused to the outside world, investing even her mediocre films with a sense of privilege that comes from our watching a performance that she habitually deemed unworthy. For us, it is not – or very, very seldom. If Garbo could not stand the sight of herself in her films, which is why preview-going was a painful obligation and viewing the daily 'rushes' one she always rejected, then for us the problem is sometimes in pardoning the film, rarely the performance.

Was she a great *actress*, though? To ask that question is to misunderstand the nature of movies. To answer it would be an irrelevant 'Yes'. Yes, she was a great actress: but she did not need to be. 'Star acting' is a contradiction in terms: some stars do not act, many actors are not stars. 'Star being' is a more cumbersome but authentic description of Garbo. Garbo, in essence, did not ever seem to need to act; yet few actresses played so many roles because she showed us so many parts of her being, physical, sexual, cerebral and purely emotional. She held a pure instinct for the part (and whichever *part* of the part she was playing) in reserve behind the eyes until the camera was turning and the lights

ABOVE Rare picture of a goddess using public transport: but the security exit was seldom far away.

OPPOSITE The safest refuge, beyond reach of age: in the light and shade of the cinema screen.

NOTES TO THE TEXT

1 Quoted in *The Kindness of Strangers* by Salka Viertel (Holt, Rinehart and Winston, New York, 1969), p. 271.
2 *Motion Picture*, June 1932.
3 *Photoplay*, April 1928.
4 Quoted in *Garbo*, by Fritiof Billquist (Arthur Barker, London, 1960), p. 10.
5 Quoted in *Garbo*, by John Bainbridge (Muller, London, 1955), p. 38.
6 *Here Lies the Heart*, by Mercedes de Acosta (André Deutsch, London, 1960), p. 232.
7 *Ibid.*, p. 216.
8 *Photoplay*, May 1928.
9 *A Memo from David O. Selznick*, selected and edited by Rudy Behlmer (Macmillan, London, 1973), p. 343.
10 *On Cukor*, by Gavin Lambert (G. P. Putnam's Sons, New York, 1972), p. 109.

11 Bainbridge, *op. cit.*, p. 109.
12 *Ibid.*, p. 109.
13 *Fun in a Chinese Laundry*, by Josef von Sternberg (Secker & Warburg, London, 1965), p. 209.
14 de Acosta, *op. cit.*, p. 217.
15 *Star Acting*, by Charles Affron (E. P. Dutton, New York, 1971), p. 130.
16 Bainbridge, *op. cit.*, p. 129.
17 Profile by Virgilia Peterson Ross, *The New Yorker*, 7 March 1931.
18 Quoted by Rilla Page Palmborg, *Photoplay*, September 1930.
19 William Sorensen, *Sunday Express*, 5 June 1955.
20 Quoted by Paul Hawkins, *Screenland*, June 1931.
21 *We Barrymores*, by Lionel Barrymore as told to Cameron Shipp (Peter Davies, London, 1950), p. 201.

22 *Kiss Kiss, Bang Bang*, by Pauline Kael (Calder & Boyars, London, 1970), p. 275.
23 *Photoplay*, December 1933.
24 Lambert, *op. cit.*, p. 114.
25 *Billy Wilder in Hollywood*, by Maurice Zolotow (W. H. Allen, London, 1977), pp. 83–84.
26 *Motion Picture*, January 1933.
27 Behlmer, ed., *op. cit.*, p. 371.
28 *Self-Portrait with Friends*, by Sir Cecil Beaton (Weidenfeld & Nicolson, London, 1979), p. 202.
29 Walter Lucas, *Sunday Express*, 8 September 1949.
30 Lambert, *op. cit.*, p. 158.
31 William Sorensen, *Sunday Express*, 3 July 1955.
32 Beaton, *op. cit.*, p. 179.

FILMOGRAPHY

Author's Note
The following list includes the principal credits of the advertising shorts and full-length features which Garbo made in Europe and America. The MGM archives have yielded some figures relating to the cost of the Hollywood productions and, rather than clutter up the text with these, I have preferred to add them to this filmography. (The accounting system of the talkie era unfortunately makes such figures, which should interest the film historian, less readily accessible.) I have also included production details, such as title changes, which I think throw valuable light on the workings of the studio.

I have left all the figures in dollars; but British readers may find it useful to remember that the official dollar–sterling rate of exchange for the period covered was: 1920: $3.54; 1925: $4.87; 1930: $4.87; 1935: $4.93; 1940: $4.03. The equivalent sterling purchasing power of $100 was respectively: 1920: £63; 1925: £65; 1930: £72; 1935: £77; 1940: £75.

EUROPEAN

1 Advertising Shorts

In 1921, Garbo appeared in *How Not to Wear Clothes*, an advertising film produced by Hasse W. Tullbergs and directed by Captain Ragnar Ring for the PUB department store, Stockholm; in 1922, she appeared in a publicity film for the Stockholm Consumers' Co-operative Association produced by Fribergs Filmbyra and directed by Captain Ragnar Ring. It is believed she also played small, unidentified (and unrecognizable) bit parts in a couple of Swedish feature films produced in the same year.

2 Luffar-Petter (Peter the Tramp)

Written, produced and directed by Erik A. Petschler.
Cast: Fire Lt. Erik Silverjälm (Erik A. Petschler); Max August Petterson, alias Luffar-Petter (Erik A. Petschler); Greta (Greta Gustafsson); Artillery Captain (Helmer Larsson); Policeman (Fredrik Olsson); Tyra (Tyra Ryman); Wife of Mayor (Gucken Cederborg)
Première: Stockholm, 26 December 1922.

3 Gösta Berlings Saga

Director: Mauritz Stiller
Scenario: Stiller and Ragnar Hyltén-Cavallius from the novel by Selma Lagerlöf
Photography: Julius Jaenzon
Production company: Svensk Filmindustri
Cast: Gösta Berling (Lars Hanson); Majorskan Samzelius (Gerda Lundeqvist); Major Samzelius (Otto Elg-Lundberg); Melchior Sinclaire (Sixten Malmerfelt); Gustafva Sinclaire (Karin Swanström); Marianne Sinclaire (Jenny Hasselqvist); Countess Martha Dohna (Ellen Cederström); Countess Ebba Dohna (Mona Martenson); Count Henrik Dohna (Torsten Hammeren); Countess Elizabeth Dohna (Greta Garbo)
Première: Stockholm, Part I: 10 March 1924; Part II: 17 March 1924

Stiller cut both parts into a single film for the Berlin première in September 1924. Some years after his death, when Sweden was short of 'sound' films, the screenwriter Hyltén-Cavallius produced yet another version by cutting Stiller's from 4,554 metres to 2,775 metres and synching music on to it from wax discs. Not till 1955 did the original photographer locate the cut footage and restore the film to approximately Stiller's intention.

4 Die Freudlose Gasse (exhibited in the United States as The Street of Sorrow; in Britain as The Joyless Street)

Director: G. W. Pabst
Scenario: Willy Haas from the novel by Hugo Bettauer
Photography: Guido Sieber
Production company: Sofar Film
Cast: Councillor Rumfort (Jaro Furth); Merchior Street Butcher (Werner Krauss); Maria Lechner (Asta Nielsen); Greta Rumfort (Greta Garbo); Frau Greifer (Valeska Gert); Lt. Davy (Einar Hanson); Regina Rosenow (Agnes Esterhazy); Rosa Rumfort (Loni Nest)
Running time: 90 minutes
Première: Berlin, 18 May 1925

AMERICAN

All the following films were produced by Metro-Goldwyn-Mayer.

1 The Torrent

Director: Monta Bell
Scenario: Dorothy Farnum from the novel by Blasco-Ibanez
Photography: William Daniels
Cast: Don Rafael Brull (Ricardo Cortez); Leonora Moreno (Greta Garbo); Remedios (Gertrude Olmstead); Pedro Moreno (Edward Connelly); Cupido (Lucien Littlefield); Dona Bernarda Brull (Martha Mattox); Dona Pepa (Lucy Beaumont); Don Andreas (Tully Marshall)
Running time: 75 minutes
Première: New York, 21 February 1926

Purchase of book: $25,000; total scenario cost: $7,528.68; total studio cost: $250,443.27. Filming began 27 November 1925, ended 23 December 1925.

2 The Temptress

Director: Fred Niblo, who replaced Mauritz Stiller
Scenario: Dorothy Farnum from the novel by Blasco-Ibanez
Photography: Tony Gaudio
Cast: Robledo (Antonio Moreno); Elena (Greta Garbo); Manos Duros (Roy D'Arcy); Marquis Fontenoy (Marc McDermott); Canterac (Lionel Barrymore); Celinda (Virginia Brown

Faire); Torre Blanca (Armand Kaliz);
Josephine (Alys Murrell)
Running time: 95 minutes
Première: New York, 10 October 1926

3 Flesh and the Devil

Director: Clarence Brown
Scenario: Benjamin Glazer from
Hermann Sudermann's novel, *The
Undying Past*
Photography: William Daniels
Editor: Lloyd Nosler
Cast: Leo von Sellinthin (John Gilbert);
Felicitas von Rhaden (Greta Garbo);
Ulrich von Kletzingk (Lars Hanson);
Hertha Prochvitz (Barbara Kent); Uncle
Kutowski (William Orlamond); Pastor
(George Fawcett); Leo's Mother
(Eugenie Besserer); Count von Rhaden
(Marc McDermott)
Running time: 95 minutes
Première: New York, 9 January 1927

Purchase of book: $7,000; total scenario
cost: $23,342.06; total studio cost:
$372,618.21. Filming began 9 August
1926, ended 28 September 1926.

4 Love

Director: Edmund Goulding, who
replaced Dimitri Buchowetsky
Scenario: Frances Marion, from Leo
Tolstoy's novel, *Anna Karenina*
Editor: Hugh Wynn
Photography: William Daniels
Cast: Anna Karenina (Greta Garbo);
Vronsky (John Gilbert); Karenin
(Brandon Hurst); Seresha (Philippe de
Lacy); Grand Duke (George Fawcett);
Grand Duchess (Emily Fitzroy)
Running time: 80 minutes
Première: New York, 29 November 1927

Purchase of book: $16,000; total scenario
cost: $32,504.95; total studio cost:
$487,994.88. Filming began 22 June 1927,
ended 25 July 1927.

5 The Divine Woman

Director: Victor Seastrom
Scenario: Dorothy Farnum, from Gladys
Unger's play, *Starlight*
Photography: Oliver Marsh
Editor: Conrad Nervig
Cast: Marianne (Greta Garbo); Lucien
(Lars Hanson); M. Legrande (Lowell
Sherman); Mme. Pigonier (Polly
Moran); Mme. Rouck (Dorothy
Cumming); Jean Lery (John Mack
Brown); Gigi (Cesare Gravina); Paulette
(Paulette Duval)
Running time: 80 minutes
Première: New York, 14 January 1928

Purchase of property: $13,000; total
scenario cost: $27,404.06; total studio
cost: $266,817.14. Filming began 28
September 1927, ended 7 November
1927. No print of this film can at present
be located.

6 The Mysterious Lady

Director: Fred Niblo
Scenario: Bess Meredyth, from Ludwig
Wolff's novel, *War in the Dark*
Photography: William Daniels
Editor: Margaret Booth
Cast: Tania (Greta Garbo); Karl
(Conrad Nagel); General Alexandroff
(Gustav von Seyffertitz); Col. Raden
(Edward Connelly); Max (Albert
Pollett); General's Aide (Richard
Alexander)
Running time: 90 minutes
Première: New York, 4 August 1928.

Purchase of book: $2,380.95; total scenario cost: $37,121.70; total studio cost:
$336,973.22. Filming began 8 May 1928,
ended 13 June 1928.

According to a studio memo, *The
Mysterious Lady* was considered 'too
ordinary' a title for a Garbo film; a
suggested alternative was *Vienna Nights*.
Howard Dietz replied that it was too late
to change the title and, anyhow, he
thought the original one as good as the
alternative.

7 A Woman of Affairs

Director: Clarence Brown
Scenario: Bess Meredyth, from Michael
Arlen's novel, *The Green Hat*
Photography: William Daniels
Editor: Hugh Wynn
Cast: Diana (Greta Garbo), Neville
(John Gilbert); Hugh (Lewis Stone);
David (John Mack Brown); Geoffrey
(Douglas Fairbanks, Jr.); Sir Montague
(Hobart Bosworth); Constance (Dorothy
Sebastian)
Running time: 90 minutes
Première: New York, 19 January 1929

Purchase of book: $50,250.00; total
scenario cost: $10,217.07; total studio
cost: $328,687.77.

8 Wild Orchids

Director: Sidney Franklin
Scenario: Hans Kraly, Richard Schayer,
Willis Goldbeck, from an original screen
story by John Colton
Photography: William Daniels
Editor: Conrad Nervig
Cast: Lillie Sterling (Greta Garbo);
John Sterling (Lewis Stone); Prince de
Gace (Nils Asther)
Running time: 100 minutes
Première: New York, 30 March 1929

Purchase of story: $10,336.64; total
scenario cost: $31,768.98; total studio
cost: $322,312.12.

The original title was *Heat*; not till
production was well advanced did it occur
to the makers that to announce 'Greta
Garbo in *Heat*' would be open to misunderstanding.

9 The Single Standard

Director: John S. Robertson
Scenario: Josephine Lovett, from Adela
Rogers St Johns' novel
Photography: Oliver Marsh
Editor: Blanche Sewell
Cast: Arden Stuart (Greta Garbo);
Packy Cannon (Nils Asther); Tommy
Hewlett (John Mack Brown); Mercedes
(Dorothy Sebastian); Ding Stuart (Lane
Chandler); Anthony Kendall (Robert
Castle); Mr Glendinning (Mahlon
Hamilton); Mrs Glendinning (Kathlyn
Williams)
Running time: 73 minutes
Première: New York, 27 July 1929

10 The Kiss

Director: Jacques Feyder
Scenario: Hans Kraly, from an original
screen story by George M. Saville
Photography: William Daniels
Editor: Ben Lewis
Cast: Mme. Irene Guarry (Greta
Garbo); André (Conrad Nagel); M.
Guarry (Anders Randolf); Lasalle
(Holmes Herbert); Pierre (Lew Ayres);
Durant (George Davis)
Running time: 65 minutes
Première: New York, 15 November 1929

Feyder was the author of the original
story, but for personal reasons he did not
want his name to appear twice on the
credits; he therefore suggested that
MGM should substitute the name
'George M. Saville'. It was originally
called *Secret Places* and then *Jealousy*.

11 Anna Christie

Director: Clarence Brown
Scenario: Frances Marion, from Eugene
O'Neill's play
Photography: William Daniels
Editor: Hugh Wynn
Cast: Anna (Greta Garbo); Matt Burke
(Charles Bickford); Marthy (Marie
Dressler); Chris (George F. Marion);
Johnny the Priest (James T. Mack);
Larry (Lee Phelps)
Running time: 74 minutes
Première: New York, 14 March 1930

A German-language version, running 82
minutes, was directed by Jacques Feyder
and premièred in Cologne on 22 December 1930. Garbo spoke her own dialogue again, and new players in the principal roles included Hans Junkerman
(Matt Burke), Theodore Shall (Chris) and
Salka Viertel (Marthy), appearing under
her maiden name as Salka Stearmann.

MGM took more elaborate pains over
the filming of *Anna Christie* than its
frequently stage-bound air suggests. Eddie Mannix, Mayer's aide, received an
anxious cable from the Coast while he was
in New York urging him to 'make sure our
sound truck is not shipped back [to
California] before we can take exterior

scenes for *Anna Christie*'. (It was then the practice of studios, coping with the problems of the talkies, to use newsreel trucks to cope with the task of recording sound on location.) The cable went on to inquire: 'Is there a reasonably priced intelligent director available in New York at the moment who could take three scenes with doubles for us?' Mannix suggested five names and recommended Bob Flores.

12 Romance

Director: Clarence Brown
Scenario: Bess Meredyth, Edwin Justus Mayer, from Edward Sheldon's play
Photography: William Daniels
Editors: Hugh Wynn, Leslie F. Wilder
Cast: Rita Cavallini (Greta Garbo); Cornelius van Tuyl (Lewis Stone); Tom Armstrong (Gavin Gordon); Harry (Elliott Nugent); Susan van Tuyl (Florence Lake); Miss Armstrong (Clara Blandick); Beppo (Henry Armetta)
Running time: 76 minutes
Première: New York, 22 August 1930

13 Inspiration

Director: Clarence Brown
Scenario: original screen story and script by Gene Markey
Photography: William Daniels
Editor: Conrad Nervig
Cast: Yvonne (Greta Garbo); André (Robert Montgomery); Delval (Lewis Stone); Lulu (Marjorie Rambeau); Odette (Judith Vosselli); Marthe (Beryl Mercer); Coutant (John Miljan); Julian Montell (Edwin Maxwell)
Running time: 74 minutes
Première: New York, 6 February 1931

Total scenario costs: $48,636.50; total studio cost: $417,379; filming began 15 October 1930, ended 24 November 1930.

The film had an unexpected commercial set-back. As the MGM legal files tell it, Gene Markey's scenario was based on a treatment by James Forbes which, in turn, drew upon Alphonse Daudet's novel, *Sappho*. The novel was public domain material in America, but still protected in some European countries. After the film had been playing in Europe for a few months, Pathe charged infringement of their ownership of the film rights to the novel. An amicable settlement was ultimately reached, but the film had to be withdrawn for a time.

14 Susan Lenox: Her Fall and Rise (exhibited in Britain as **The Rise of Helga**)

Director: Robert Z. Leonard
Scenario: Wanda Tuchock, from the novel by David Graham Phillips
Dialogue: Zelda Sears, Leon Gordon, Edith Fitzgerald
Photography: William Daniels
Editor: Margaret Booth
Cast: Susan Lenox (Greta Garbo); Rodney (Clark Gable); Ohlin (Jean Hersholt); Burlingham (John Miljan); Mondstrum (Alan Hale); Mike Kelly (Hale Hamilton); Astrid (Hilda Vaughn); Doctor (Russell Simpson)
Running time: 75 minutes
Première: New York, 15 October 1931

As mentioned in the text, *Susan Lenox* was first banned by the British film censor, then passed with 125 feet of film cut out of it and the proviso that the title be changed so as not to be associated with a 'scandalous' book. Thalberg suggested *Forbidden*, *The Stain* and *The Daring Lady* as alternatives before MGM's London office produced the acceptable *The Rise of Helga*.

15 Mata Hari

Director: George Fitzmaurice
Scenario: original screen story and treatment by Benjamin Glazer and Leo Birinski
Dialogue: Doris Anderson, Gilbert Emery
Photography: William Daniels
Editor: Frank Sullivan
Cast: Mata Hari (Greta Garbo); Lt. Alexis Rosanoff (Ramon Novarro); General Shubin (Lionel Barrymore); Adriani (Lewis Stone); Dubois (C. Henry Gordon); Carlotta (Karen Morley); Caros (Alec B. Francis); Sister Angelica (Blanche Frederici)
Running time: 90 minutes
Première: New York, 31 December 1931

In addition to the problem, mentioned in the text, of showing an execution, British censorship was worried by the implication that the Novarro character preferred a profane love for Garbo to the sacred watchfulness of the Virgin Mary on the wall ikon. Thalberg offered to film a retake, using a picture of the boy's mother with a lamp burning under it in place of the ikon and eliminating all religious implication. The censors could not agree: the mother would have to be in contemporary clothes to please them. They did agree, however, to retaining part of the execution scene to which the dialogue referred. For a time, therefore, the film, as exhibited in Britain, had a couple of very slight jump cuts until Thalberg's alternative material arrived to be incorporated in the print.

16 Grand Hotel

Director: Edmund Goulding
Scenario: William A. Drake, from Vicki Baum's play
Photography: William Daniels
Editor: Blanche Sewell
Cast: Grusinskaya (Greta Garbo); Baron von Gaigern (John Barrymore); Flaemmchen (Joan Crawford); Preysing (Wallace Beery); Otto Kringelein (Lionel Barrymore); Senf (Jean Hersholt); Meierheim (Robert McWade); Zinnowitz (Purnell B. Pratt); Pimenov (Ferdinand Gottschalk); Suzette (Rafaella Ottiano); Chauffeur (Morgan Wallace); Gerstenkorn (Tully Marshall)
Running time: 105 minutes
Première: New York, 12 April 1932

MGM acquired the rights to Vicki Baum's play for $13,500 and had a profit participation in the New York production as well. Filming began 30 December 1931, ended 19 February 1932, with retakes completed by 29 March 1932. Total studio cost was $695,341.20. Studio records throw illuminating light on the proportion of the production costs charged to each of the stars, their relative standing, and the good balance of interest maintained in terms of screen time: Garbo: $68,000; Crawford: $60,000; John Barrymore: $55,750; Beery: $55,500; Lionel Barrymore: $25,000; Stone: $17,812; Hersholt: $3,364.

No fewer than five writers worked (uncredited) on *Grand Hotel*'s scenario: this was now becoming the practice as Garbo vehicles grew more ambitious and costlier.

17 As You Desire Me

Director: George Fitzmaurice
Scenario: Gene Markey, from Pirandello's play
Photography: William Daniels
Editor: George Hively
Cast: Maria/Zara (Greta Garbo); Count Bruno Varelli (Melvyn Douglas); Carl Salter (Erich von Stroheim); Tony Boffie (Owen Moore); Mme. Mantari (Hedda Hopper); Lena (Rafaela Ottiano); Baron (Warburton Gamble); Captain (Albert Conti)
Running time: 71 minutes
Première: New York, 2 June 1932

18 Queen Christina

Director: Rouben Mamoulian
Producer: Walter Wanger
Scenario: Salka Viertel, H. M. Harwood, from an original screen story by Viertel and Margaret F. Levine
Dialogue: S. N. Behrman
Photography: William Daniels
Editor: Blanche Sewell
Cast: Queen Christina (Greta Garbo); Don Antonio de la Prada (John Gilbert); Magnus (Ian Keith); Chancellor Oxenstierna (Lewis Stone); Ebba Sparre (Elizabeth Young); Aage (C. Aubrey Smith); Prince Charles (Reginald Owen); French Ambassador (Georges Renevent); Archbishop (David Torrence); General (Gustav von Seyffertitz); Innkeeper (Ferdinant Munier); Christina as a child (Cora Sue Collins)
Running time: 97 minutes

Première: New York, 26 December 1933
Total scenario cost: $103,904.11; total studio cost: $1,127,479.63. Filming began 9 August 1933, ended 24 October 1933.

19 The Painted Veil

Director: Richard Boleslawski
Producer: Hunt Stromberg
Scenario: John Meehan, Salka Viertel, Edith Fitzgerald, from W. Somerset Maugham's novel
Photography: William Daniels
Editor: Hugh Wynn
Cast: Katrin Fane (Greta Garbo); Walter Fane (Herbert Marshall); Jack Townsend (George Brent); General Yu (Warner Oland); Herr Koeber (Jean Hersholt); Frau Koeber (Beulah Bondi); Mrs. Townsend (Katherine Alexander); Olga (Cecilia Parker); Amah (Soo Yong); Waddington (Forrester Harvey)
Running time: 83 minutes
Première: New York, 7 December 1934

20 Anna Karenina

Director: Clarence Brown
Producer: David O. Selznick
Scenario: Clemence Dane, Salka Viertel, from Tolstoy's novel
Dialogue: S. N. Behrman
Photography: William Daniels
Editor: Robert J. Kern
Cast: Anna Karenina (Greta Garbo); Vronsky (Fredric March); Sergei (Freddie Bartholomew); Karenin (Basil Rathbone); Kitty (Maureen O'Sullivan); Countess Vronsky (May Robson); Stiva (Reginald Owen); Yashvin (Reginald Denny)
Running time: 95 minutes
Première: New York, 30 August 1935

21 Camille

Director: George Cukor
Producer: Irving Thalberg
Scenario: Zoë Akins, Frances Marion, James Hilton, from the novel and play, *La Dame aux camélias*, by Alexandre Dumas *fils*
Photography: William Daniels
Editor: Margaret Booth
Cast: Marguerite (Greta Garbo); Armand (Robert Taylor); M. Duval (Lionel Barrymore); Nichette (Elizabeth Allan); Nanine (Jessie Ralph); Baron de Varville (Henry Daniell); Olympe (Lenore Ulric); Prudence (Laura Hope Crews); Gaston (Rex O'Malley); Gustave (Russell Hardie); Saint Gaudens (E. E. Clive); Henri (Douglas Walton); Corinne (Marion Ballou); Marie Jeanette (Joan Brodel); Louise (June Wilkins); Valentin (Fritz Lieber, Jr.); Mlle. Duval (Elsie Edmonds)
Running time: 109 minutes
Première: New York, 22 January 1937

22 Marie Walewska (exhibited in the United States as Conquest)

Director: Clarence Brown
Producer: Bernard H. Hyman
Scenario: Samuel Hoffenstein, Salka Viertel, S. N. Behrman, from a novel, *Pani Walewska*, by Waclaw Gasiorowski and a dramatization by Helen Jerome
Photography: Karl Freund
Editor: Tom Held
Cast: Marie Walewska (Greta Garbo); Napoleon (Charles Boyer); Talleyrand (Reginald Owen); Captain d'Ornano (Alan Marshal); Count Walewska (Henry Stephenson); Paul Lachinski (Leif Erickson); Laetitia Bonaparte (Dame May Whitty); Prince Poniatowski (C. Henry Gordon); Countess Pelagia (Maria Ouspenskaya)
Running time: 115 minutes
Première: New York, 4 November 1937

The film cost over $3 million, a huge sum for those days, and corporate uncertainty over which audience it was aimed at is reflected in the dizzying series of changes undergone by the title. Believing *Marie Walewska* too much of a mouthful for the American box-office, Howard Dietz, early in May 1937, proposed changing it to *Flame of the Century* or, in descending order of preference, *The Woman Before Waterloo*, *Star-Crossed*, *Less Than the Dust*, *Sands of Glory*, *No Man Is God*. Frank Whitbeck, of MGM's New York office, in turn proposed *The Gods and the Flesh* or *Dusk of Empire*. By 14 June, as it was still unresolved, Whitbeck suggested *The Captains and the King*, *Symphony Without Music*, *The Great Surrender*, *The Road to Waterloo*, *Where Is the Glory?*, *A World Is Born*, *Glory*, *The Immortal Sin*. On 23 June, Dietz replied from the Coast that this outburst of alternatives was 'not popular'. On 28 June, Whitbeck cabled that there had been a good response at his end to *Before Waterloo*, but he believed this could still be improved on. He suggested *The Night Before Waterloo*. This was approved. But by 9 July, F. L. Hendrickson, head of MGM's contracts department on the Coast, wanted to change the title to *Conquest*. This was discovered to have been registered already by Warner Bros. Warners waived their objection on 23 July, and Jack L. Warner personally traded it off for a title held by MGM, *Man Without a Country*, which, he added tongue in cheek, knowing the huge budget of the Garbo film, he wanted to use 'for a two-reel historical subject'. *Conquest* was finally registered on 26 July, but only for North America. A fresh argument now ensued over whether the more sophisticated European market should get the full title *Marie Walewska* or, simply, *Marie*. The former won.

Seventeen writers, including Donald Ogden Stewart, appear to have had a hand in the screenplay at one time or another.

The MGM files show that the studio had a vexatious couple of years following the release dealing with claims from authors who alleged they had submitted treatments in earlier years or asserted they could detect similarities between their version of Napoleon's love-affair and the film's.

23 Ninotchka

Producer-director: Ernst Lubitsch
Scenario: Charles Brackett, Billy Wilder, Walter Reisch, from an original screen story by Melchior Lengyel
Photography: William Daniels
Editor: Gene Ruggiero
Cast: Ninotchka (Greta Garbo); Count Leon d'Algout (Melvyn Douglas); Grand Duchess Swana (Ina Claire); Iranoff (Sig Rumann); Buljanoff (Felix Bressart); Kopalski (Alexander Granach); Commissar Razinin (Bela Lugosi); Count Rakonin (Gregory Gaye)
Running time: 110 minutes
Première: New York, 9 November 1939

Ninotchka, on which ten writers worked, also underwent a series of title changes. The first, suggested in March 1939, was *We Want to Be Alone*; Howard Dietz warned that this would evoke 'a bad reaction' – no one needed to guess from whom. For a long time after shooting began on 6 June, it remained simply 'the Garbo film'. By July, the studio suggested *Give Us This Day*. From the New York office, J. Robert Rubin replied flatly, 'None of us here likes *Give Us This Day*.' *A Kiss from Moscow* was put forward as an alternative. Dietz replied in August, 'I am afraid there is a subtle bigotry these days which would extend to mention of Moscow in a main title. I am afraid on Main Street they might say, "If it's from Moscow, we don't want any part of it." In my opinion, *Intrigue in Paris* is a great title.' Some time after this, *Ninotchka* was proposed, but not settled on. At the end of August, Frank Whitbeck reeled off a string of alternatives: *This Time for Keeps*, *The Love Axis*, *Time Out for Love*, *A Kiss for the Commissar*, *Salute for Love*. Bernie Hyman suggested *A Foreign Affair* or *A Kiss in the Dark*. Eventually Nicholas Schenck, president of Loew's Inc., which owned MGM, himself Russian by birth, intervened and issued a ukase: it was to be *Ninotchka*.

Though *Ninotchka* began production before the outbreak of the war in Europe, company correspondence indicates how delicate MGM realized they needed to be regarding the treatment of the Russians, particularly if co-operation had to be sought from the Soviet Union. Thus a production executive from the studio cabled MGM's New York office on 3 June 1939, asking for aid in obtaining a shot of Red Square, which was wanted for use in a series of dissolves. This was put in hand with the advice, 'Suggest you resist any request to read the script'. Requests were also made, underlining the need for reticence, too, for shots of 'interior Russian apartment-house staircases' and 'interior apartment where several people sleep in one room'. The attitude of censorship in Britain was particularly problematical, in view of the country's political policy of appeasement, and Sam Eckman wired the studio on 24 May 1939: 'No previous censorship experience Soviet story, but hope censor will consider this a comedy, otherwise will prove troublesome. Many Russian films depicting Soviet ideals rejected, but suggest keeping Communistic angle in mind, also that Turkey is friendly country, and Russia may become one.' The war settled such doubts.

24 Two-Faced Woman

Director: George Cukor
Producer: Gottfried Reinhardt
Scenario: S. N. Behrman, Salka Viertel, George Oppenheimer, from a play by Ludwig Fulda
Photography: Joseph Ruttenberg
Editor: George Boemler
Cast: Karin (Greta Garbo); Larry Blake (Melvyn Douglas), Griselda Vaughn (Constance Bennett); O. O. Miller (Roland Young); Dick Williams (Robert Sterling); Miss Ellis (Ruth Gordon); Miss Dunbar (Frances Carson); Dancer (Bob Alton)

Running time: 94 minutes
Première: New York, 31 December 1941

Two-Faced Woman cost a modest $316,000, evidence, perhaps, of how MGM were cutting their budget according to their (remaining) world market. It, too, suffered the by now endemic title changes. When Garbo signed a five-page contract to make the film, on 20 November 1940, it was called *I Love Your Sister*. Just before production, *The Twins* was substituted, then *Anna and Anita*. Other titles followed thick and fast: *Her Naughty Sister, Her Weekend Sister, Her Wicked Sister, Naughty Today and Nice Tomorrow, Nice Little Hussy, It's Nice to Be Naughty*. The studio liked *Her Sister's Husband* best, but the song in the film, *I Can't Remember Your Name*, was also a favourite. *Double Meaning, A Double Life* and *Beside Herself* were canvassed. By 14 September, the studio was considering *Her Sister's Husband, The Gay Twin, The Adorable Twin, Her Gay Sister*. Eddie Mannix suggested *Happily Married, Twin Wives, The Shadow Wife, One-Day Bride*. The final title *Two-Faced Woman* was suggested by Howard Dietz; it was also the title of a song he had written with Arthur Schwartz. It was registered in September 1941, less than two months before the film was released, and then abruptly withdrawn, following the Roman Catholic National Legion of Decency's criticism of its moral content,

to be re-presented with editing cuts and other changes on the last day of the year.

Retakes for the additional scene, making it clear the Melvyn Douglas now realized that the 'twin' was his wife, were directed by Andrew Marton and Charles Dorian. Other changes were made in the editing so as to eliminate 'the attitude to marriage that the picture now carries'. Among the lines that disappeared were: 'How does my position affect your position?' – 'Because we're related'; 'Let's drink to what's in our minds'; 'You must have been born in the tropics'; 'Are you all things to all men?'; 'You international trollop!' The footage of 'the couch scene' was reduced; so was a shot of Garbo in a low-cut dress. In a letter to Eddie Mannix, dated 10 December 1941, J. Robert Rubin commented: 'When the [new] scene is inserted in the picture, and the audience clearly understands that Blake knows that Katherine is his wife Karin, it is possible that certain pieces of this dialogue and these scenes will right themselves. . . . You may however have to cut scene showing her toenails, which in the picture indicates the time when he recognizes her as his wife.' Rubin also counselled that the Press release state that the reason given for agreeing to the Legion changes was 'maintaining right moral standards in the entertainment produced by this company'.

BIBLIOGRAPHY

Garbo has attracted biographers and essayists from an early stage in her career. The following list is by no means exhaustive.

Bainbridge, John: *Garbo* (Muller, London; Doubleday, New York, 1955; updated edition, Galahad Books, 1974). The best general life.

Beaton, Sir Cecil: *Self-Portrait with Friends* (ed. Richard Buckle, Weidenfeld & Nicolson, London, 1979). Selections from Beaton's diaries, 1926–1974, bringing together his various encounters with Garbo. By far the most intimate view of the star.

Billquist, Fritiof: *Garbo: A Biography* (Tr. Maurice Michael, Arthur Barker, London, 1960). View of Garbo by one of her countrymen, also an actor; good on the early life.

Corliss, Richard: *Greta Garbo* (Pyramid, New York, 1974). One of the most stimulating critical looks at her films.

Crowther, Bosley: *Hollywood Rajah* (Holt, Rinehart and Winston, New York, 1960). A biography of Mayer that sheds useful light on his relations with Garbo.

Durgnat, Raymond & Kobal, John: *Greta Garbo* (Studio Vista, London, 1965). Small but lavishly illustrated study.

Sjolander, Ture: *Garbo* (Harper & Row, New York, 1971). Excellently designed photo-biography.

Tyler, Parker, Michael Conway *et al.*: *The Films of Greta Garbo* (Citadel, New York, 1963). Sprightly and provocative introductory essay by Tyler.

Works in foreign languages are almost as numerous as those in English. Among the noteworthy publications: Ducout, Françoise: *Greta Garbo, La Somnambule* (Stock; collection *Femmes dans leur temps*, Paris, 1979); Lernet-Holenia, Alexander *et al.*: *Greta Garbo: Ideal des Jahrhunderts* (Limes Verlag, Wiesbaden, 1937); Montesanti, Fausto: *Greta Garbo* (Canesi, Rome, 1965).

Among the books and periodicals containing critical essays on Garbo are: *American Film*, vol. 1. no. 1 (Oct. 1975), David Robinson: 'Garbo in Retrospect'; *Films in Review*, vol. 2. no. 10 (Dec. 1951), Theodore Huff: 'The Career of Greta Garbo'; *Focus on Film*, no. 15 (Summer 1973), DeWitt Bodeen: 'Memories of Garbo'; *Sight and Sound* vol. 23. no. 4 (April/June 1954), Kenneth Tynan: 'Garbo' (reprinted in *Curtains*, Longmans, London, 1961); *Sight and Sound*, vol. 28. no. 1 (Winter 1958/59), Louise Brooks: 'Gish and Garbo, the executive war on the stars'; *The Silent Picture*, no. 16 (Autumn 1972), Robert Cluff: 'Garbo's Hollywood Silents'; *Garbo and the Night Watchmen*, ed. Alistair Cooke (New ed., Secker & Warburg, London, 1971); *Kiss Kiss, Bang Bang*, Pauline Kael (Calder & Boyars, London, 1970; Little, Brown & Co., Boston, Mass., 1968); *The Celluloid Sacrifice* and *Stardom: The Hollywood Phenomenon*, Alexander Walker (Michael Joseph, London, 1966, 1970).

INDEX

ILLUSTRATION SOURCES

The majority of the photographs reproduced in this book are the copyright of Metro-Goldwyn-Mayer, Inc., and have been supplied by their picture archives at Culver City or by the Margaret Herrick Library, Academy of Motion Picture Arts and Sciences. The rest of the illustrations are supplied or reproduced by kind permission of the following:

Ahlén & Akerlunds Förlags 12 (top), 21 (bottom), 26–7, 31 (top and bottom right), 36 (bottom), 37, 88 (top), 124, 152 (bottom right), 166 (bottom), 172 (top), 173 (top and bottom), 176 (bottom), 177 (left), 180

Cecil Beaton, courtesy of Sotheby's Belgravia 162, 167, 168–9, 171 (top and bottom)

British Film Institute 30, 34 (top)

Kevin Brownlow 58–9

Camera Press 179

Sven Gustafsson front and back jacket, frontispiece, 66–7

Kobal Collection 10, 44 (top), 45 (top), 178

Pressens Bild 108 (right), 152 (bottom left), 164; (photo Olle Lindeborg) 165, 166 (top), 172 (bottom), 174 (top), 175 (top)

Swedish Film Institute 12 (bottom), 13 (top and bottom), 14 (top and bottom) 15, 16 (top and bottom), 17 (top and bottom), 18–19, 20 (top), 21 (top), 24 (top and bottom), 25 (bottom), 29, 38 (top), 88 (bottom), 89, 174–5, 181

Weidenfeld & Nicolson Archive 8, 19 (bottom), 20 (bottom), 23, 25 (top), 31 (bottom left), 68, 101

The caricature by Einar Nerman (177 top), from the book *Caught in the Act*, is reproduced here by permission of George Harrap & Co., Ltd.